Social Media Millions:

Your Guide to Making Massive Amounts of Money
from Social Media Selling

By Ryan Stewman

Social Media Millions:
Your Guide to Making Massive Amounts of Money
from Social Media Selling

All Rights Reserved

ISBN-13: 978-1717425454
ISBN-10: 1717425453

Cover design by Sooraj Mathew

HARDCORE RESOURCES

SOCIAL MEDIA

Facebook
277,000 followers
Fan: www.facebook.com/hardcorecloser
Sales Talk With Sales Pros Group:
www.facebook.com/groups/salestalk
Personal: www.facebook.com/realryanstewman

Twitter
16,300 followers
Personal: www.twitter.com/ryanstewman
Business: www.twitter.com/hardcorecloser

LinkedIn
12,400 followers
Personal: www.linkedin.com/in/ryanstewman
Business: www.linkedin.com/company/hardcorecloser

Instagram
119,000 followers
Personal: www.instagram.com/ryanstewman

Business: www.instagram.com/hardcorecloser

YouTube

3.5 million views/10M minutes watched

www.youtube.com/user/ryanstewman

Snapchat

ryanstewman

Skype

ryanstewman

PODCASTS

THC Podcast

Top 50 Business Podcast on iTunes, 50K listeners

Get Your Mind Right Podcast

Top 50 Business Podcast on iTunes, 50K listeners

BEST-SELLING BOOKS

- *Sell It and Scale It: How to Transition from Salesman to CEO* (2017)

- *F*ck Your Excuses: The Misfit's Guide to Avoiding Upper Limits* (2017)

- *Elevator to the Top: Your Go-To Resource for All Things Sales* (2016)

- *Bulletproof Business: Protect Yourself Against the Competition* (2016)

- *Kick Ass - Take Names, Emails and Phone Numbers* (2015)

- *Hardcore [c]loser*, A Top Business Book of all Time, Amazon (2015)

WEBSITES

Hardcore Closer Blog

500,000 Visitors Monthly

www.HardcoreCloser.com

Articles, Digital Products, Training Resources

Break Free Academy

www.BreakFreeAcademy.com

Funnel Closers

www.FunnelClosers.com

Phone Sites

www.PhoneSites.com

Clyxo

www.Clyxo.com/Closer

Table of Contents

Introduction

Social Media Millions isn't some "rah rah" hype, beast of a book. It's filled with step-by-step instructions on how to make money from social media. It's not some theory I read somewhere either. It's firsthand experience that's helped me make eight figures from selling on social media.

Each chapter of this book is independent of the next. Each chapter is a separate learning lesson. Some of the chapters are industry-specific, but if you're smart, you'll figure out how to use the same tactics in your industry.

I started out using social media posts to prove to an ex-wife that I wasn't a loser and in fact, that she was the one who'd lost. From those posts, people reached out to me asking for help. At the time I was doing mortgages. I had just gotten out of federal prison, and I lost my wife while locked up. I posted my victories and client testimonials on Facebook just in case she decided to see what I was up to. Those posts led to more business from my "friends" online. This was in 2008.

After doing this for two years and then losing my financial license due to being a federal criminal, I started my own social media agency. In 2012, I took on over 70 clients, and I made 2-5 posts a day on their behalf. That's right; I wrote over 350 posts a day for my clients. Because of this, I gained a lifetime of social media expertise and experience.

In 2013, I decided it would be a helluva lot easier to teach what I know than to continue to post 350+ times a day. I began to teach professionals how to leverage social media to make money. This was during a time when people did not treat social media like they do today. Most people thought Facebook and other sites were a fad and a waste of time.

Despite these objections, I changed the doubters' minds and proved that social media was more powerful than traditional media. This was before 99% of the social media stars and gurus you know had even caught on. Some of those clients I wrote posts for have gone on to build nine and 10-figure per year businesses.

The principles and strategies you will learn from this book are simple. After all, we must remember Keeping It Simple Sales (KISS), but smart people tend to overcomplicate the simple things in life. However, the simple things work the best, so don't try to reinvent the wheel here. Instead, go with what I teach you and make it work for you.

Take action on what you learn in this book, and you WILL see results. Remember, though; nothing happens overnight. Your audience may judge you, make fun of you, and try to get you not to do what I'm teaching, but after a month or so they will be proud of you, and tell everyone they know you.

Learn this stuff, do it and make millions from it. That's the plan, and that's the reason I wrote *Social Media Millions*. Let's get after it!

Chapter 1:

Social Media Prospecting is the New Digital Door-2-Door

I live in Dallas, Texas and if you go around the neighborhoods here knocking on doors, you risk getting a gun pulled on you. It's 2018, and no one likes uninvited visitors knocking on their doors. Matter of fact, in most of the areas around here, door-to-door (D2D) is illegal unless you have a permit from the city, which is a bitch to acquire.

I'm not gonna lie, though, when I started off doing mortgages, I would drive around in the evening knocking on doors of homes for sale, talking to the homeowners about getting a mortgage from me. That was in 2003, over 15 years ago. Even back then, I had to knock a lot of doors to get an application. The internet was brand new and social media wasn't even in the MySpace phase yet.

Nowadays, if you knock on doors, the prospect knows you're desperate, new and don't have any leads.

I've never once in my life bought anything other than Girl Scout cookies from anyone who's knocked on my door. I'm not saying D2D doesn't work; I'm saying it's inefficient AF. Even in 2003 when I knocked doors, it was because I had no leads or prospects.

There's an easier way that D2D salespeople seem to simply ignore out of sheer hard-headedness. Old habits die hard. We live in the modern age of internet leads, online prospecting and social media. It makes ZERO sense to walk around random neighborhoods knocking on doors of strangers.

I already know what some of you reading this think: *But I sell roofs. I sell alarms. I sell X.* You can sell all that faster, better and more efficiently using the online methods I'm about to share with you. D2D is dying off, and online prospecting is going harder than ever before. It's just a matter of changing how you look at things.

Let's say you sell roofing. The typical roofing salesman goes door to door after a hailstorm offering free roof inspections. In places like Texas, this is nothing new;

we see it all the time. The thing is, D2D folks have to wait until the storm is over and hit the hood the next day. What I teach my roofers to do is run a geo-targeted ad on Facebook and Google offering the same free inspection and discount on repairs if needed. The ad goes up in 10 mins during the storm. Guess what? When the electricity goes out in a storm, people get on their phones on social media to kill time.

Let's say you sell alarms D2D. Instead of knocking on doors, I'd use Facebook groups to connect with Realtors and loan officers. After all, they are the ones who sell houses and have access to the most recent buyers in the area. I'd work out a referral program with those agents and have them send me every deal they close, so I can keep their clients safe.

Old-school thinking is way too common these days. Innovation always wins. Efficient innovation wins even more. While old-school sales tactics have people walking D2D; digital prospecting is knocking hundreds of doors per second. You tell me which one is most likely to get more deals closed.

I know what you're thinking, though. You say things like "But I'm a closer face-to-face," and you might be but if you are a one-dimensional salesman, you will be left behind soon by those of us who can close face-to-face, on the phone, over text, and through video and ads. If you're only good face-to-face, you need to expand your sales skills.

Chapter 2:
Hate Traditional Networking? Try This Online Method Instead

If you're like me, you most likely hate traditional networking, because let's just be honest, this is what happens. You show up at an event where you don't know anybody, hoping you can get business from strangers, which if you think about it, is absolutely crazy. Why? Because no stranger with a ton of business is sitting around trying to figure out how to give their tons of business to other strangers. So, what really happens when you show up at a networking event is: you expect somebody else to have business; you find out they don't have any business, and they expected you to have business, and then they find out that you don't have any business. It turns out that neither one of you have any business networking because you don't have a network to share amongst each other anyway.

Well, it can be frustrating for both parties. It can be frustrating for everybody.

I've seen a lot of people start up network groups and then let the groups crumble because none of the members had any value to give. A bunch of leeches and a bunch of bloodsuckers showing up at these networking events are never going to give any leads away, but they're always going to try to take leads from other people. Any time you put multiple folks in a scenario of that magnitude, where they're just trying to get business from each other instead of giving value to each other, it's not going to work out.

You don't really have a choice on who you can connect with when it comes to the traditional networking groups. You don't know who's going to be at the next meeting, especially if you're showing up to a new one. You also don't know the caliber of person who's going to be there.

If you hate all of that, I've got good news for you.

There is a better way. You see, right now, you can go to sites like Facebook, Snapchat, Instagram and LinkedIn, and send a friend request. You can follow or send a friend request to any person you want. In the time you'd spend driving back and forth to traditional networking events where you're not going to get any business from anyone, you could give value trying to get to know somebody on a social media site. In today's day and age, people consider their friends online to be just as close as their friends offline. If you translate that concept to the business world, your network online is just as powerful as your network offline.

I urge you to try the Lucky 7 Method instead.

The Lucky 7 Method Works Like This:
(Before you get started, remember to be strategic about the people you're engaging.) These are the three steps to the Lucky 7 Method: First, write on somebody else's wall. Second, send a direct message to one person, and third, seven days a week, leave a comment on somebody else's post.

If you did that three times a day, seven days a week for an entire month, you'd have contacted 93 different people in your network, and if you choose correctly, the ones that you'll have interacted with would be the ones you'd most likely get business from. So, if you're tired of traditional networking, if you're tired of the roaches and leeches trying to get business from you that you don't have in the first place, try the Lucky 7 Method. We call it the Lucky 7 Method, because it makes a lot of people lucky, seven days a week.

Chapter 3:
Creating a Social Media Syndicate

Do you have at least 100 friends on Facebook? Of course, you do. Even the catfish spammers with hot chick profile pics from Thailand have 100 friends. The average FB user has 338 friends. Since you're reading this, you're above average which means you most likely have 1,000 friends or more.

Are you doing any business with those 1,000 friends?

Facebook is a noisy place. With almost two billion user profiles, there are a lot of variations that are considered before a post hits the newsfeed. This means that unless your posts are viral and super engaging, only about 70 of your 1,000 connections ever see your posts. But what about the other 930 people?

Imagine another 930 people seeing, engaging and being indoctrinated by your posts. What would that mean for your business? Do you think you could get some leads out of the extra exposure? Of course, you could!

In order to reach the maximum amount of friends you're connected to as possible, you need to create what I call a "social syndicate." Your five best friends or five best referral partners can really get some massive coverage in the newsfeed if you all work together and conspire to take common action.

Chapter 4:

How I Made $500,000 in Sales This Year from FREE Facebook Groups

Let's go into great depth about how I built my Sales Talk With Sales Pros group on Facebook and the steps I took to grow it. Once I go over the four basic strategies it takes to grow the group; I'll tell you how you can monetize the following you've built in the group.

The Four Basic Strategies for Growing a Facebook Group:

1. Create a Club:
Design content that helps the members. Your group isn't for everybody; you want people to feel like they are privileged to be a part of an elite club. Just like any exclusive club, there are rules. For example, if you go to a nightclub, you will see a dress code. You will also see people who were invited to attract others. Make sure to bring influencers into your group, too.

2. Remember Culture: Take the "ure" out of "culture" and think about creating a cult. Our entire society is built around cults. You can establish this atmosphere by using your own language that other people who are not in the club won't know. There are no ads in the group, and so you can be the advertiser and influence your cult.

3. It's Us Vs. Them: This is the understanding that you are better than your competition who are posers. We are the ones who work hard and are on frontlines. Whatever your industry, make sure your group stands out as people who are authentic, who do the work.

4. Be Benevolent with Your Talents: Offer group-only bonuses, so your tribe will see how much value you will bring them. Give value that only you can give so the members of the group will appreciate you. Running exclusive offers for groups can be very profitable for you, as well. People know they better purchase what you are offering because they can't get it anywhere else.

The size of the group does not matter. I know admins who run groups with 100,000 members, but they make no money because they don't do it right. On the flip side, I know people who have 500-person groups who make $20,000 per month from them. It's all in how you run the group. I just happen to run a large one.

If you're not using Facebook groups to grow your business, you're missing out on some seriously awesome leads from people who know, like and trust you.

Chapter 5:
How NOT to Make Sales from Facebook Groups

As the admin of the largest sales-related group on the largest social media site in the world, I know a thing or two about selling products to members of Facebook groups. My main group, Sales Talk With Sales Pros has over 74,000 active members, and they are ALL real people.

About three years ago, I started the STWSP group, and I wanted it to be a different place than all the other groups out there.

As a direct result of being the admin of that group, I've made seven figures in gross product sales. It's taken a lot of trial and error to get my pitch/process down to a science.

I see a lot of people in my groups and the groups of others making big mistakes. What people don't realize is that spam is spam. The thing about spam is that some people don't even know they are spamming.

When I started my blog, I would post links to the blog in other people's Facebook groups. An admin once accused me of spamming, and I didn't realize that just because I knew my site wasn't spam, no one else did. Therefore, I got kicked out of several groups for doing just that.

Nowadays, I see members of my groups doing the same thing. It makes logical sense. Share a link, get some engagement is the plan but that's not how it works. If you post a link to an unknown site in a FB group, just know that your post looks like spam. Especially if you just posted a link and didn't write any text to go along with it.

Chapter 6:

Here's How I've Personally Made Millions of Dollars Running Facebook Ads

Before we start, I'm not really the braggy type. I just know there's a lot of vague, bullshit ads out there telling you, you can get rich from Facebook and I want to stand out because I don't talk about it. I AM about it. In 2016 alone, I spent $256,000 and some change on Facebook ads. This was my personal money and not some shit I managed for a client either.

What you're about to get from me is real talk.

Over the last three years, I've hired no less than four Facebook experts to run my ads. Not a single one of them has gotten the results I have. I'm not knocking these people; I'm just saying I got this FB ads game figured out. No one has been able to get the reach, click costs or any other metrics, to the levels I take them. I'm about to tell you how I do it.

Also, I want you to know that I'm not doing targeted list segmentation or using any kind of fancy software that requires an Ivy League education to operate. I've turned a quarter million in FB ads to over two million dollars by keeping it simple.

My process is easy and highly effective. Which means you will have a high probability of not doing anything you're about to read here. Smart people, like the people reading this book, tend to knock simple shit and think surely, it's more complicated than it seems. I promise you it isn't.

My first time running Facebook ads was in the beginning of 2013. My buddy, AJ Roberts helped me run my first ad. It was a simple video with a Wufoo link for people to fill out if they wanted to learn more. That 4-step funnel generated over $50,000 in three weeks with just $2,500 in ad spend.

It was at that point I decided I loved FB ads just like a junkie loves heroin.

After continuing to run ads and profit from them, I reached out to Josh Flagg from *Million Dollar Listing LA*. My (then) partner and I worked out a deal with Josh to host a Million Dollar Mastermind. It was a success. Josh, the partner and I made a few dollars after it was all said and done.

After my time with Josh ended, the partner reached out to Fredrik Eklund, and we did the same thing, only WAAAY bigger and faster. It was the first time I had hit a 6-figure return from FB ads. This was in 2013, the year BEFORE *MDL NY* was nominated for an Emmy. During the time I ran those ads, they went from last place on Bravo to first. I contributed to the awareness of the show.

The Million Dollar Program was working great, but it was up to the celebrity to keep it going. I was literally at the mercy of the celebrity, and you know how finicky they can be, especially when they are busy making millions of dollars in real estate sales. I had to turn over my ownership in the company to the partner and set off on a trail of my own. This was in 2015.

I then started running FB ads to my blog HardcoreCloser.com, and it began gaining in popularity. When we have an ad blitz going on, the site will get a half a million visits in a month. The fan page on FB has 177,000 fans, and the IG fan page has 114,000 followers. So, I've done the experiments to gain the experience and become the expert.

I'm ready to share my expertise with you.

It all starts with three equally important parts. Each of these parts can't be overlooked. If you leave one out or don't finish one, your entire ad/funnel/system will not work. I've seen so many people fail at running ads because they don't have the trifecta triangle (these three things) in place.

First, is your offer. You need a strong offer that commands attention and solicits an answer. I like to use the following formula. "Would you like to get X without having to do Y?" X = What they want. Y= What they don't want. This formula is simple and super powerful. For example, in real estate, we run ads that say, "Would you like to be the first to know when new houses hit the market without getting bombarded with emails every day?" The simpler the better.

This formula is important because it asks. When your ad asks a question, it demands an answer. It's human nature. They have to answer it. This is how you get the attention and get them to qualify themselves. Some people want it. Some don't. Everyone who sees it makes the decision. Also, your picture, video, image, or whatever you share visually is part of the offer. Make sure it matches the words in the ad.

Second, you need an audience. The right audience/offer combo is the ONLY way you will make money from FB ads. You can have the greatest offer in the world, but if you put it in front of the wrong audience, you won't sell a thing. The offer is the first step. Now, we have to choose who the right person for the offer is. That's where the targeting comes into play.

I like to keep my audiences limited to 100,000 people or less when I'm spending $100 per day, per ad. If you spend $100 and you have the right targeted audience, you will reach them. For my real estate company, I run local ads. For my sales training and seminar companies, I run ads all over the world. You need to decide who will take you up on your offer, then target those folks with the offer to be sure they will.

In my experience, it's best to keep hitting the same audience over and over. Familiarity goes a long way. You'd do better to tweak your offer in front of the same audience than you would to find new audiences. Also, FB will optimize your audience for who is most likely to click, but it takes a few days of data to do so.

Third, you need a funnel that converts. If you have an awesome offer, the perfect audience and a broken funnel, you won't make money. I like to make an offer that goes to a landing page that collects their first name, email address and mobile phone number. The mobile phone number is so I can text them.

I use a 4-step funnel that is super easy. FB ad >> Landing Page >> Thank You Page >> Like on FB

Basically, I make a post and boost the post. That post has a call to action to click a link to my landing page. On my landing page, the offer is reinforced and hammered harder. When they opt in, they get what was offered. While on the thank you page, the call to action is "Like us on Facebook" with a button linked directly to my page. I drop them off where they started, back on Facebook.

With these three parts, that I call "the trifecta triangle" you can easily run ads that convert.

If you have a simple, clear offer, you will convert. People scroll Facebook quickly, so your ad needs to stand out. Ask them a simple question they can answer to make a decision.

I run 3-5 ads at once. Plus, I post 3-5 times a day organically on my fan pages. I'm producing a ton of content to drive traffic, eyes and organic exposure to my offers and ads as well. That's what's great about FB ads. You can get "free" exposure, too, if the ad is good.

After each of the ads has been running for three days, I shut down or tweak the weaker ads. The ones which cost more per click, get less exposure or don't convert, get tweaked or cut. Every day I log in to FB, check my ads, see which ones are performing and turn them up. The ones that are not performing, I turn off. Remember, do this every single day.

Chapter 7:
Why You Should Be Focusing on Facebook Groups

There is a lot of noise on Facebook these days. Even though the smart folks over at FB corporate are working hard to dumb it down for us simple people, there is still a lot of noise to sift through. As often happens with noise, you miss out on the things you want to hear, due to the noise over-noising it. Thanks to noise on Facebook, I miss people's important updates that I really want to see. So, how do you tone down the noise? I'm finding a great deal of success with small Facebook groups. Generally speaking, thanks to EdgeRank, your affinity of active friends is a small circle anyway. Why not use a group for all of your communication needs? Facebook groups are actually very functional these days and easy to assemble and use. More and more businesses and charities are using Facebook groups to keep in touch with a target audience for a specific cause. You can communicate and connect on a more intimate level with people of your choice.

Facebook groups can be super small to super big.

In countries outside the USA, FB groups have led revolutions. Matter of fact, FB groups were responsible for the Arab Spring. If using a simple concept like groups on Facebook can overthrow a government, think of what it can do for your business.

Your clients can spread the good news about you like wildfire!

If you are not using Facebook groups as a part of your marketing plan, you could be missing out on connecting with your prospects and partners on a deeper level.

To learn more about this topic, watch my video on How to Set Up Facebook Groups on HardcoreCloser.com

Chapter 8:

You Only Get One Shot to Make a BIG First Impression on Facebook

It's amazing to me how many people do not have the "about" section on their Facebook profile filled out correctly. When a new person, i.e., a potential client or connection, hits your page for the very first time, they immediately take a look at the "about" section right under your Facebook profile picture. That small box sums you up in very few words. We all know there are billions of dollars changing hands all over Facebook. Honestly, I don't know the numbers, but it wouldn't surprise me if there were more business done on Facebook than on LinkedIn.

With that in mind, why wouldn't you want your "about" section to POP OUT and grab your new visitors' attention to draw them in to read more about you?

For those of you who already do this, double check to make sure your work history and your company's business page are linked. Once someone is there to know more about you if they click on your work page and see it's a "blank" page, it's not a good first impression. There are more than double the amount of people on Facebook than are on LinkedIn. Many of us have these detailed LinkedIn "about me" sections but terrible looking Facebook "about" sections. If there is twice the traffic on Facebook, then why not be sure to put twice the effort into making that first impression on Facebook?

It's 2018, and the game has not changed, it's merely on!

If you don't get ahead of the competition or at the very least, catch up to your competition, you will not only get left behind, you will go out of business. I watched an episode of *48 hours* yesterday where random ladies tracked down a killer and gathered evidence, just by using Facebook. If you don't think your friends and clients are looking you up on there from time to time, you are mistaken.

This is why you should always keep your house clean when you are popular because you never know who will stop by. So, if you are popular or trying to be popular on Facebook, you better keep your profile in top shape. You don't have to do a bunch of work; just make sure you fill in all the blanks and that your job history links to the right pages. If you use or plan on using Facebook to prospect for leads and clients, then you need to be sure they can "get to know you" the right way before they click away, forever missing the opportunity to give you their money.

Here are the three sections that MUST be filled out properly on Facebook if you want to look like you are competent.

The most important: You must have your "works at" section linked up correctly. The days of catchy titles that lead to blank pages are over. Have your real work history go to either your business page or to your fan page. If your business does not have a page, shame on them/you. Go make one right now.

The second most important to-do: The "about you" section on your profile should have not only personal stuff but business achievements and what you are good/bad at as well. This is the one shot you get to connect with a new visitor when they are trying to see who you are and what you do. That's what we Americans do; we ask who you are and what you do. Make sure you address both of these questions clearly in your "about you" section.

Last but not least: Where you live is key. It does not matter where you live, but it matters that you live somewhere. People want to know where you are from, so they can try to connect with your roots somehow in their own way and mind. Be sure to fill this section out. Even if you live in La Jolla but list your residence as San Diego, that's cool because it shows you live somewhere. No one gives business deals to the homeless.

There you have it. I've given You enough reasons why and removed all the reasons why not. So, go fix your profile and have the answers ready when new visitors show up with questions about you. In all my years as an online marketer, I've learned that simplicity is the key. You don't need a bunch of fancy sites or crazy web traffic schemes to make money. You only need clarity and advice from an expert who has been there and done it before. I've run the experiments to gain the experience to become the expert I am today.

Chapter 9:
3 Benefits of Using Facebook Check-Ins for Your Business

In case you have been locked in a dark hole, ("It puts the lotion in the basket") then you are aware that Facebook has a "check-in" feature. That easy-to-use, simple, Facebook check-in can make a BIG difference in how you run AND market your business. I'd like to share with you how I have been coaching small and large businesses alike, to utilize the Facebook check-in feature for all it's worth.

You don't have to be a social media expert to understand and see the power behind what I am about to share with you. You can implement these practices into your business tomorrow and with no costs or additional staff needed.

1. Raving Fan Customers:
The #1 and most obvious reason to utilize the Facebook check-in button is to get customers to share your brand with their friends. This not only spreads the word about your business, it shows the people who the

word is spreading to, that there are other people happy with you. There are two ways to entice a customer to use the Facebook check-in feature while at your place of business. Number one: You can simply ask them. This is by far the most effective way to make them check in. Number two: Give them an incentive, i.e., a free gift or discount to check in. Either way, your brand will grow organically.

2. Employee Advocates:
Having your employees share the times when they arrive and leave work has a HUGE impact on your Facebook branding. Some employers have a hard time asking their employees to use their Facebook for business purposes, but in my opinion, if they want a job, they will do what needs to be done. If the average employee has around 400 Facebook friends and they check in at your store five times a week, that is pretty powerful [FREE] branding for you. If you have two or more employees, you can do the math exponentially.

Another benefit of your employees using the Facebook check-in feature is the social proof it provides to others that your employees are proud to be sharing your brand. Businesses that have happy employees attract more customers.

3. Managing Your Employees' Time:

From a management space, think of the stealthy way you can use Facebook check-ins to see what time your employees arrive on location and/or leave work. Not only do you get the branding and advertising, you also get to make sure that they are where they are supposed to be when they are supposed to be there.

If you want more information about the Facebook check-in feature and how it can benefit Realtors in particular, watch my video on HardcoreCloser.com: Mobile Facebook Marketing Strategy for Realtors

Chapter 10:

The Best Way to Post on Facebook to Get Comments

The whole idea of social media is to be social, right? So, why not try to be the center of attention? The more eyes on you, the more chances you have to fill a need. There is a shift going on with Facebook right now, as I write this. Facebook is changing the way posts show up in peoples' timeline.

The most engaging posts consist of words and a picture, and if possible, you will see people have been tagged. You absolutely don't want to post a picture without words, or words with no pictures. Resist posting a link and nothing else. I promise if you do this, you will get fewer likes and engagements.

Another effective posting method is to ask a question that people will be interested in answering. When you do this, you allow them to use their own thoughts and responses, and people appreciate that. Whatever you post, make it compelling so followers will want to talk about it.

Finally, always like people back and let them know their comments and feedback are appreciated.

Chapter 11:

Converting Your Social Media Friends and Followers into Paying Customers

Just because a person has a massive following online doesn't mean shit. I know plenty of social media celebrities who don't even earn six figures a year. Sure, online they look and act like ballers. In reality, they may have a lot of eyes on them, but eyes don't always equate to dollars.

However, I know plenty of people with small followings online who do $1-2 million in revenue per month.

Yes, you read that right, "per month." It's not about the size of the following you have; it's about the dollars you can ethically extract from your followers. At least that's all that matters to me. Don't get me wrong, I love to inspire and motivate people in my sphere of influence, but I'm in this game to make money. Without it, I'd be simply wasting time on social media.

Looking the part ain't shit. Faking it 'til you make it, is for people who care more about appearances and approval than money. Consider this, when you see some of these gurus spend their last dollar on a Tesla or exotic car; Jeff Bezos drives a Honda Accord. Why? Because Bezos has fuck-you money and could give a shit what you think about him. Look, I own nice cars and shit, too, but I bought them *after* I was a millionaire, not so I could look like one. When I was coming up, I leased an Infiniti Q50 for $400/month. It was a great car, too.

If you're in the social media marketing game, the key is to get money from your following, not to keep feeding them value while hoping, wishing and praying your connections will think highly enough of you to give you their money. If that's your plan…newsflash! They won't do it. Nope, people will keep their hand out waiting for more of your free shit until you die. Stop feeding kangaroos and convert them into clients!

I've made over $7,000,000 from Facebook and Instagram alone. The IRS can verify this because they have the tax checks to prove it. I mention my earnings because I want you to know that what I'm about to say is not speculation or theory, it's a fucking fact, and I've personally done it. On top of that, I have clients who have had 6-figure months from social media.

So, how do you convert friends and followers into paying customers?

First, you need a product or service to sell, and you can't be afraid to sell it. Approaching the sale requires a delicate balance, though. Meaning, you need to market on posts and sell via comments and DMs. Most people never understand this. While it's okay to sell via posts, it's not the most effective way to close. People like a personal touch and to feel like you personally sold to them. Closing people is easiest to achieve through comment replies and direct messages.

Today, for example, I made a post on Facebook that I was taking DMs from my friends who wanted to talk about how my programs could help them. I made over $20,000 in less than two hours. All from DMs hidden from the public eye. I keep my shit out of the public eye because roaches always find a way to make weak attempts to roach your salivating buyers from you. They poach your posts and attempt to railroad your prospects. I've got my game on lockdown, so if people want to know how it's done they gotta hit me up personally and go through the process. Some people won't reach out because they are scared I will close them.

I follow the simple 80/20 rule and don't deviate: "Create 80% content and posts for THEM aka your audience, and 20% posts for ME aka my business and sales." Then I share four posts that make them laugh and teach them lessons. On the fifth post, I ask them to take some sort of action that leads us to doing business together.

I don't have to flash my cars, watches, homes or any of that shit to close prospects.

Instead, I add value by offering what I call "subliminal pitches" every day. Subliminal pitches include testimonials and stories about those who have worked with me and are seeing success. I do this from a lesson-learned standpoint, not as a direct pitch.

I see people who use their pages to constantly pitch products and programs and those people rarely get engagement. If you are going to rack up sales, people need to see your posts. If your posts are not engaging, Facebook won't show them in the newsfeed and friends will have no idea what you are selling.

You have to be creative, and you have to be engaging.

In my group, Sales Talk With Sales Pros, now over 74,000 members strong, and with 240,000+ engagements per month, I use the 80/20 rule and have my team do the closing via comments and DMs. They watch my posts and close. Period. No one sees me work my magic and they never suspect my team is out there making them dolla' dolla' billz, y'all.

If you're on social media to be popular, that's cool, but if you use it to make money, you gotta post, prospect and close. There's no way around it. If you fight the process and worry about running people off, then you're never gonna make it. If they get mad you've offered to help them, are they really worthy of following you in the first place?

If you read my posts and comment on my shit every day, then I hit you up and ask you to join one of my programs, and you get all butt hurt, that says more about you than it does me. I'm all for giving value to people, but I'm also all about closing sales. That's the game I'm enrolled in, and I show up to play it every day. I'm going to ask for the business, if not today or tomorrow, it will be soon enough.

Chapter 12:

7 Ways to Make Sales on Social Media
(Even with Only 500 Followers)

It's easier than ever to get leads and close sales from social media. While a lot of people are complaining about the changed algorithm and so forth, you are staring at the biggest opportunity in history to make sales at a rapid pace. Just a decade ago, your only choices for sales were cold calling, networking and door knocking. Now, with over four billion people using social media, you can make sales without ever meeting, or even speaking to prospects.

I first made money from social media in 2009. I was fresh out of federal prison, and I had ZERO prospects in my pipeline. I started doing some of the things I'm about to share with you and making sales. I was doing millions of dollars in mortgage business from Facebook alone.

That's when I knew I had found a better way.

Flash forward, and I've been teaching people how to make money from social media for over nine years. I've helped multiple people become millionaires from social media sales. Almost everyone I've helped to make money on social media has had to start from scratch. That means no mass popularity and nothing but hard work to build a following from nothing.

Most people want to know where to start and how to find "new" people to connect with so they can sell them something. When most people wake up to the social selling revolution, they realize they only have close friends and family as connections and they need some real prospects fast.

Here are seven ways you can make sales on social media no matter if you have a big following or not.

1. Groups:
Groups are the best places to find leads and connections on social media. Think about it; groups are niche interest segments of the internet. If you are selling to real estate investors, there are hundreds of

groups full of thousands of members for you to join, engage and close in.

Strategy:

Find a group to join and instead of posting and spamming, engage with other posters in their comments. Reach out to the admin and ask what the group needs that you maybe can help with. Get to know the top posters, the group influencers and the active commenters. Treat groups like rooms of people who are perfect fits for what you sell.

2. Search Bar:

Search bars on social media sites are grossly underused. Mostly because people think they can only search for profiles. In reality, social media search bars filter all the content on the site for you. It's literally a Google of the entire network, with every post and profile. The better you get at using the search bar, the more leads you'll find.

Strategy:

Go to your social media site of choice and type in quotations and phrases like "buying a car in Dallas," and it will bring up all the people who've posted about buying a car in Dallas. From there, you can comment or DM them to see if they have bought yet or not. Search for phrases on social media that your prospects might post about but put them in quotations.

3. Influencer Pages:
Influencers are easy pages to get leads from. Leaders like Gary Vee, Tony Robbins, Eric Worre and Dan Bilzerian have like-minded people following them. These pages have millions of followers and can't keep up with people commenting. The comments on their posts are filled with people asking for help. The influencer most likely won't help them but you can.

Strategy:
Figure out what influencers your prospects follow and follow them as well. Turn on the notifications and every time they post, sift through the comments. When you find someone who needs your help, reply to their comment (with value, not a pitch) and start a conversation with them.

4. Marketplace:

Only a few social sites have this feature right now. It's social media's version of Craigslist. In the marketplace, people sell all sorts of stuff. From guns to cars to TVs and houses. You can trust the people in the marketplace a little more than Craigslist because FB does a good job verifying profiles.

Strategy:

Look through the marketplace and see who's selling stuff that would trigger them to need what you sell. If they are selling a TV, car or house, chances are they need another one. Go sell them what they need to be sold.

5. Find Friends:

This is a feature on sites like Facebook, Twitter, LinkedIn and Instagram. It matches users up with other users the algorithm deems compatible. In other words, it's saying "Here's someone you should connect with." If you are bold enough, send a few of those people who look qualified, a request every day. Do some social recon on them first, though.

Strategy:

Go to your friend finder and send a request to a few people. Once they accept, send them a message thanking them for connecting. Nothing creepy. Maybe even add some value for them. Be cool, just as if you'd met someone in real life. Once you make the first impression, keep communicating over time to create familiarity, sales and referrals.

6. Events:

Events are much like groups in that they are both great for connecting with like-minded people. Think of events as groups with expiration dates. Events have lots of people posting, RSVPing and interacting. Events are great places to find people who fit your prospect profile.

Strategy:

If you know a big event is coming near you, find the event on social media and join it. Then engage in the comments, make posts and connect with like-minded people who you feel are a good fit for your following. Look for BIG events so you can connect with the event coordinator, etc.

7. Live Video:

Most social media sites offer live video right now. It's the most popular thing on social media as of the time I write this. Social sites are pushing live videos and quality video content really hard right now. Plus, video gives you a real live look into how someone lives, acts or works.

Strategy:

Do a live video once a week and ask your network to comment, share and like your video. While you are recording the live video ask them to engage, invite cool people and share your video. It's like automatically getting referrals from your perfect prospects.

Chapter 13:

How to Generate Coaching and Consulting Leads from Social Media

Look, I'm not about to share some elaborate money-getting scheme here. I've proved that you don't need any of that. I'm the guy who continuously yells at my tech guy to dumb things down.

You see, the problem with smart people, like you, the person reading this, is that you're too damn smart for your own good. Pair that up with ego, and it's a combination for coaching destruction. I'm about to share something ultra-simple and easy to implement. Your natural tendency will be to knock it and discredit it as being "too easy." I assure you, that if you choose to think that way you are giving yourself a major setback.

I've built a multi-million-dollar consulting business from social media. A large majority of my leads, sales and clients come directly from sites like LinkedIn and Facebook. I've spent the last nine years of my life working audiences and prospecting on social media.

It's safe to say I know a thing or two about generating leads.

I'm mostly known for helping salespeople but when you think about it, pretty much everyone, including you, is in sales. We all sell something; that's how we pay our bills. Until recently, I've never talked about or taught anything to coaches like you, who are trying to build an empire. So, this is literally the first look at behind the scenes of how I've pulled off what I have.

The very first thing you need to figure out is who you want to consult or coach. It's not "anyone who wants to X." That's unacceptable. Coaching clients want accountability and customization. People have "special" and specific things they need help with. You have to get your perfect prospect dialed in.

For example, when I started off in the coaching world, I taught only loan officers. First off, I knew the business and spoke the language. Second, I was really good at it and had the track record. I ran ads that specifically spoke to mortgage officers only. Anyone who was a LO knew I was an insider and everyone who wasn't a LO was confused AF. I was 100% clear on who it was I wanted to help.

I see so many talented coaches losing deals to BS coaches all the time because they aren't clear on EXACTLY who it is they serve.

If you're not clear on this, go to YouTube and search "Frank Kern Core Influence" then watch Frank take you through the perfect client equation.

Once you get your perfect prospect figured out, you need to make a list of 25 of those perfect prospects. We call this the "Dream List" and it's the top 25 people you'd love to have as clients. If you don't know 25 people you'd like to coach, out of your thousands of Facebook friends and LinkedIn connections, you maybe shouldn't be in coaching. Just sayin'.

Now that you have a list of your top 25 prospects go to their Facebook page and select "get notifications" so that you'll be notified every time they post on "The Book." Your job is to engage, gain familiarity and build trust with these 25 people through Facebook. Every time they post, you get a notice, then you go leave a comment. Let them know you exist.

Now that you know exactly who it is you can and want to help, it's time to craft an offer to match the audience.

An offer needs to follow this simple formula. "How to get X without having to give Y." Remember, X= what they want and Y= what they don't want.

When I started out and sold to LOs, my offer was "How to go from $2 million per month in mortgages to $5 million without hiring a team, paying for leads or recruiting a ton of Realtors." Another was "How to get business from real estate agents without kissing ass and buying all their leads for them."

At this point, if you've followed my multi-million-dollar advice, you've got a prospect, an offer and all you're missing is a way to collect lead information. If you read my article on The Simplest 4-Step, Lead-Generating Funnel Ever on HardcoreCloser.com it will tell you step-by-step how easy it is to set up the funnel.

Now you have a funnel, a list of prospects to go after and an offer to hit them with.

So, all you have to do is get the offer in front of the 25 prospects. But the last thing you want to do is run them off by spamming them or constantly nagging them to let you coach them. You've got to be smoother than that.

What I do is create videos and blog posts demonstrating my expertise. If you don't have a blog, you can sign up with Medium.com for free and use it as your blog. Create content that is 80% training and 20% call to action. Post this content in groups; ask your friends to share it; post it in the comments of groups and get the word out any way you can.

If you want to speed this process up, you can create a fan page and run FB ads.
It's a quick and easy way to get leads to see your content and take you up on your call to action. After all, that's all you're trying to do. Go after your Dream List and generate cold leads from groups, etc.

Right now, we generate roughly 8,500 leads per month from social media. Most of them come from the exact process I just explained. I know you'll be quick to say, "It's too simple. My business is different," and I'm here to tell you that your business is not that special. Especially as a coach.

Let's be real though, generating leads is only half the battle. Once you get the lead, then you have to close and collect payment. After that, the pressure is on us, because we have to deliver what we promised in the beginning. Delivery of service is the most crucial part of the process. After you've gone through all of the above to get a client, the last thing you want to do is lose that client and have to start all over.

Chapter 14:

10 Ways to Generate Mortgage Leads Quickly from Social Media

My mortgage origination career ended in 2010. Leaving the mortgage business was one of the hardest things I've ever done in my life, and I've had to do some really hard things. In 2009, I closed 183 loans. By the time I left the business in March of 2010, I had already closed 77 loans.

Even in 2008, the year I discovered Facebook, I would get leads from the first HUGE social network.

I had an online social media strategy, long before it was mainstream. I'd close 3-4 deals a month just from posting on Facebook.

When I left the mortgage business, I decided to start a new life helping loan officers close loans from social media leads. In the last seven years, I've helped thousands of LOs close billions in loans from leads generated on social media sites. I'll share my top 10 ways to prospect on social media with you, but it's up to you to take action.

Top 10 Ways to Prospect on Social Media

1. Real Estate Groups:
Facebook and LinkedIn are loaded with real estate groups. My client Eli Torres has a group on Facebook called "Real Estate Happy Hour" and the LOs that frequent that group and engage, all get leads from it.

2. Send DMs Asking for Referrals:
First off, you should be connected to every client you close on your PERSONAL Facebook page. Every time you close a loan, ask them to connect. Then periodically, check in with them through DM and ask for referrals (in a cool way).

3. Search Hashtags:
Realtors love hashtags. You can search common hashtags like #realestate followed or preceded by the city you live in like this: #DallasRealEstate

These hashtags are usually loaded with agents. Hashtags work on pretty much ALL social media sites, too. You can search the same hashtags on different sites over and over.

4. Garage Sale Groups:

A garage sale is what's called a "trip wire." A trip wire sends a signal to the base that someone is in your territory. A garage sale is a signal that the homeowner is about to move. Why else would you want to reduce the amount of shit you own? Asking why people are having a garage sale is the key to pulling prospects out of these groups.

5. Share Realtor's Listings:

When you connect with an agent, and you see them share a nice listing, share it with your audience for them. This alerts the agent that you're trying to help, plus your friends may see the listing and ask you to get them a loan for it. Don't share shitty listings, though. It's bad form.

6. Lucky 7 Method:

The Lucky 7 Method is a simple way to prospect 90 people a month, without being pushy, awkward or weird. It works like this; each day, do the following: comment on one agent's post, leave a post on another agent's wall and send another agent a DM. Do this every day for 30 days, and you'll have connected and conversed with 90+ agents. I go into this method more in chapter 2 of this book.

7. Share Pictures from Closings:

When you close a loan, ask the family to take a picture of them with the papers, and send it to you. Then, post the picture, tag your clients and the agent. When you make the post, be sure to add a call to action at the end, something along the lines of: "If you'd like to be as happy as the Smiths fill out an application at…"

8. Create a Syndicate:

A syndicate is a group of people conspiring to take common action. You can get a couple of agents, a title rep, credit repair person, insurance agent and home inspector to help you comment and bump your posts.

If you share a closing picture and your syndicate shares it, you'll get 5-10X the exposure.

9. Creating Videos:

Videos, especially live ones, get a ton of exposure and engagement on social media. Video is the new public speaking. When you step out of your comfort zone and use video to attract, educate and even close prospects from social media, you're utilizing the most powerful marketing tool available right now.

10. Leaving Comments:

Have you ever noticed that you have to log in to some social media sites to leave a comment on their websites? Surfing your favorite site and leaving comments is a good way to prospect and generate leads. I used to comment daily on the KW blog, and I'd get 100+ clicks and 2-3 leads every time I left a comment.

Chapter 15:

9 Ways to Get Free Leads from Social Media

I may not know you, but I'd be willing to guess you're a pretty good salesperson. You've probably said, "Put me in front of someone, and I can close them," a time or two. I've come to notice that the biggest problem facing salespeople isn't selling, it's lead gen. You can be the best salesperson in the world, but if you don't have prospects to sell to, it doesn't matter.

I have this belief. I've run my entire business on this one belief. I believe that everyone can be a good salesperson if they can find the right thing to sell and the right people to sell to. Selling is actually the easy part of our job, but we spend 99% of our time prospecting and not selling. Getting quality leads isn't easy. Salespeople who can generate their own leads can write their own paychecks. For as much as they want.

Lead generation doesn't have to be hard, boring or expensive.

Most of us who work in sales, spend our time educating ourselves with books, programs and coaches. We get all badass at sales and then face the ultimate problem: no one to sell to. I'll show you nine ways you can get free leads from sites like Facebook, LinkedIn, Twitter and any other social media site out there. Social media leads are the best leads there are. They are ready, real and easily engaged.

9 Ways You Can Get Free Social Media Leads:

1. Posting in Groups:
In the event you don't have a vast network of social media followers, you can join groups and engage with the people posting in them. Once you get a feel for the atmosphere in the group, you can make a post. I suggest asking a question or taking a poll. Those who comment on your post are new leads for you to work.

2. Creating a Syndicate:

We discussed this in the prior chapter. The same rules apply here.

3. Asking Questions:

Social media is flooded with people who are all about themselves. When you ask a question, people love to give you their opinion. Ask the right questions, and you'll not only get engagement, but you'll get high quality leads from the commenters.

4. Engaging with Hashtags:

Pretty much every social media site uses hashtags. You can connect with like-minded strangers and even find high-quality prospects by using the right hashtags in your posts and engaging with others who've used hashtags in their posts. For example, if you sell homes, the hashtag #realestate is full of leads and prospects when you search it.

5. Commenting on Websites:

Sites like *Huffington Post*, *Entrepreneur* and *Forbes* all rely on social media sign-ins. This means when you comment on these sites; you are logged into another site and posting as that profile. You can find the hottest articles, read the comments and connect with the commenters on their respective social media profiles. It's one of the easiest ways to find leads.

6. Sharing Posts:

The most flattering thing anyone can do online is share another person's stuff. It's the ultimate social media kudos. Also, when you share someone's post, they get a notification that they don't get often. This makes you stand out and get their attention. Share someone's stuff and engage them.

7. Sending DMs:

The more you send someone DMs, the more they see your posts in their feed. The DM is the ultimate way to get in front of a prospect. I like to do what's called "social recon" and send DMs accordingly. I've made millions from leads using the DM method.

8. Creating a Quiz:

You can go to Wufoo.com, start a FREE account, create a quiz and post that quiz in a group. The people who take the quiz are leads. I've used this in sales groups. I created the Closer Quiz and I'd just drop the link into the post. We've gotten over 8,000 leads from organic group quizzes.

9. Contests:

If you've got some cool shit to give away, contests can really help you gather a grip full of leads, too. We recently gave away a package that generated 8,000 new leads for us in just 10 days. All organic, all from posting in groups and pages and having our syndicate help.

Chapter 16:

How Social Media Takes the COLD out of Cold Calling

If you say you like cold-calling, you're a got-dammed liar!!! No one likes smilin' and dialin'. They only do it because they make money from it or because they have to. Worse yet, no one likes getting cold called. It's not like anyone wakes up and says, "I'm going to buy shit from a random stranger who bothers me on the phone today." Think about it...

When cold calling, one of the biggest struggles and the first thing most salesmen strive to do is create a bond of familiarity. We attempt to find common ground with our prospect. Even if it's a love for the same sports team. We'll do anything just to work an "angle."

Cold-callers have to work 200 times harder than everyone else. First, you must get past the people who don't answer their phone. Second, you have to find common ground quickly. Third, you must work tactics to get your prospect to buy. It's a grueling process that leads to more self-loathing. The last thing a salesman needs is stress. We've got enough of it already.

Social media puts an end to all of these problems.

Ever notice that magnifying glass on every single social media site? It's called a "search bar," and you can type words in it. After you type words in it, it searches for those words on the interwebs. When you search Facebook, Twitter and Instagram for words like "real estate" or "for sale" you'll find things like real estate and shit for sale, as I've mentioned. Pretty fucking amazing, huh?

What about using the search feature to find your target prospects? If you knew what to search for you could connect with people who could use whatever in the hell it is you sell. Instead of calling hundreds to find one, you could go in like a sniper and save your bullets.

Once you search out and connect with new potential clients, don't go for the throat immediately. It's so annoying when I accept a friend request only to be spammed with a sale link five minutes later. Trust me; no one's buying shit in that fashion.

Social media mirrors real life. Just like you wouldn't meet someone for the first time and say "HEY, I HAVE STUFF FOR SALE. YOU SHOULD BUY IT. LOOK AT THIS." Don't do it on social media. As it is in real life, you have to take the time to get to know someone. Communicate with them and earn their trust. Show them you're the go-to guy when they need your shit.

Here's how to do just that…

Start treating Facebook like real life. When someone says something at a party that makes you laugh, you say, "That's funny." Do the same thing on Facebook or any SM site for that matter. When you see a post you like, like it. When you want to chime in on someone else's post, do it.

Engage.
Interact.
Be social.

After a few days of liking, commenting and engaging with someone on social media, then it's time to reach out to them via direct message. But wait. You still don't want to use the "buy my shit" scheme. We need to be more methodical if you are going to succeed at sales on social media. If you do it wrong, people will blast your intentions all over the web. If you do it right, you could pull tons of cash, by adding tons of value to the right people.

You're going to reach out to them and mention something you noticed that they posted about recently. Maybe you strike up a conversation about their favorite sports team. Maybe you mention the photo of their kid. Oh, wait, that would be creepy as fuck. Don't do that. Chris Hanson will show up on you. All joking aside, use their recent post content to gain that familiarity bond.

See. Wasn't that much easier? Being a sniper is way easier on our stress levels than being the frontline guy charging through the door with a machine gun. Besides, social media is NLP-programmed to be a positive experience. After all, you're friends, right?

People like buying from friends. A cold call comes from a stranger. No one's supposed to talk to strangers.

Chapter 17:

The Social Media Marketing Strategy of the Century

When I do simple keyword research on what to blog about, it never ceases to amaze me, some of the things people search for. They crack me up. Who teaches these "searchers" how to type in English? Sometimes when I picture someone performing searches on Google, I think they must have some sort of clef-lipped computer accent or something. No different from when you hear someone use broken English to communicate with a foreigner. "You close-y the door maybe?"

Anyway…because of this hilarious problem, I am able to search out stupid little "extras" that make all the difference in how a site is found online. One of the biggest discrepancies I notice when doing keyword searching is the word "the" is often used.

For example, "the facebook business" is a search term which makes no logical sense. Why would someone use that phrase? But apparently, hundreds of thousands do so every month. Kind of weird but totally cool.

I've been doing little tests like this for years, and nothing surprises me now. I've been doing similar tests for Facebook "keywords" (if you want to call them that) as well. And because of that, I've composed the social media marketing strategy of the century. Who knew so many open keywords were searched on Facebook every day and that no one is taking advantage of them? No one (other than me) has yet to set their mark on Facebook keywords.

"Yes," they do exist, and even though the Facebook search is annoying, it serves a good purpose, is awesome, easy-to-use and highly underrated.

To properly utilize the social media marketing tactic that I am going to share with you, it will require you to generate content and post often to your Facebook page. After all, how can anyone search for a word and find you, if you have not posted that word?

Here is a simple breakdown of the social media marketing strategy:

Step 1: Find out what your customers, audience and prospects are talking about and what kind of phrases engage them. You can do this by online stalking your peeps. (but in a cool non-violent way, lol).

Step 2: Start using those phrases and their language in your posts. Even demonstrate your insider lingo by commenting on the same fan pages and group threads where they are.

Step 3: Care about them and get to know them. Never jump in and go straight for the sales pitch. You have to grow a relationship and earn the right to ask them for business.

Step 4: Once you have created the bond, simply offer them a chance to utilize your products or services. If they say "yes," great, if they say "no," treat it as no big deal. Don't let a turn-down or rejection harm the bond you have already built. They may be back

Step 5: Repeat this process over and over on as many social media sites as possible. The more information and content you release out into internet land, the more chances there are for your prospects to find you. Do it, then do it and then do it again. Don't stop until you have all the money you want.

I'm living proof that the social media marketing world is not complicated. I believe in simple, yet highly effective online maneuvers that convert friends and fans into paying customers. You don't need elaborate web schemes or an expensive website. All you need is clarity and direction from someone who has been there and done that. My clients love me because the social media marketing tricks I teach them cost nothing and yield big results.

Chapter 18:
The 5 Social Media Prime Times

Marketing 101 taught us all to know our audience. I've taken it one step further by making my clients identify their perfect customer. You see, we waste so much time trying to cast a broad marketing net when statistics show that niche markets hold the highest conversion rates. It's easier to catch the right fish if you have the proper lure.

In my time as a high-level social media manager and consultant, I have accumulated quite a few clients. So many clients in fact that at one time my company made up to 5,000 posts in a 24-hour period throughout many different social media platforms. Since we have shifted our focus, we now make about 50 posts a day. This has given me the ability to gather analytics beyond most people's comprehension. My clients work across many different industries, but the one thing they all have in common is that they are all in sales. My clients hire me to sell stuff on their behalf using social media and the internet. Plain and simple, that's the bottom line.

I'm constantly testing and testing and testing again what works. I've taken in clients that have a Facebook account with 80 friends all the way to clients that have 30,000+ social media connections.

One of the top occurrences I see on social media after we take over an account is the familiarity factor. Most of my clients are not really active on social media. I take them from 1-3 posts a week to 3-5 posts a day. It takes their audience a month or so on average to get accustomed to this frequency. Once they do become accustomed, they become familiar and branded. This is no different than direct mail or an email branding campaign.

To do all of this without pissing my clients' friends off, I have to understand their audience, who they want to talk to, and what they are trying to accomplish. Once I get my head around those three aspects, I can set up campaigns that not only create engagement; they will convert friends to clients. If the content I create is boring, too salesy and unfriendly, I could cost my clients, customers.

With that in mind, I have discovered that there are five social media prime times. You know primetime, like on TV when the best shows come on. Yes, it works the same way on social media. In TV land, primetime is between 7-9 PM CST—only two hours a day. (at least in Dallas where I live), but in social media land, there are primetime spots for 16 hours of each day. Different times apply to a different audience.

To use them and market effectively, you must understand who is viewing, when and why. With my 10,000+ hours of extensive research and constant split testing, this is what I have come up with.

PRIMETIME SPOT #1 "EARLY RISER" 5-9 AM
The Early Riser spot is a primetime slot that I fit into. This slot is for the people who wake up, check email, Facebook, their calendar, and everything else before they get their day started. The Early Riser knows that when he/she gets the day started, there will be no time for playing on Facebook.

PRIMETIME SPOT #2 "EMPLOYEE/STAY-AT-HOME MOM" 9 AM-12 PM

This time period consists mainly of employees and stay-at-home moms (SAHM). Studies show that SAHM are more likely to surf Facebook in the morning. This is a quiet time for them and gives them the ability to have a little fun on social media before they are caught up in running the house for the day. As far as the employee goes, this is the time when a couple of things are happening. Thing #1 is the employee is driving to an office somewhere. As much as it pisses me off, people surf Facebook and drive. Thing #2 is the typical employee will get coffee, turn on a computer, surf around and waste the first 30 minutes of every workday. You and I both know that Facebook takes up a good grip of that 30-minute time period. That's why many companies have Facebook blocked. But everyone has smartphones so what good does that do?

PRIMETIME SPOT #3 "THE FOODIE" 11 AM-2 PM

Remember back in the good ol' days of Facebook when you could take a picture of your lunch and everyone would like it and comment on it? This still happens on a regular basis. People are known to surf Facebook to see what their friends are doing for lunch. Because of this trend, many people have gotten accustomed to checking Facebook before they go to lunch. This primetime slot is also a time when people are standing in line for lunch. We can admit that we ALL stare at our phones while we wait in any line. Americans will do anything to avoid eye contact with strangers these days. This is a great time to make sure your posts are mobile-friendly.

PRIMETIME SPOT #4 "AFTERNOON DELIGHT" 3-6 PM

This spot is the #1 most heavily trafficked time on social media. This is the prime time of primetimes. The people surfing during this time slot are mostly made up of two groups. Group one is made up of the employees that have finished work early for the day and are killing time before they leave. The second group contains the people all over the USA sitting in traffic. I hate to say it, but the numbers don't lie. This gives them a quick time to check social media again before going home to their family for the evening.

PRIMETIME SPOT #5 "FINISHER" 6-10 PM

This spot is for the folks who make sure everything is all in order before they call it a day. The person who is making sure all their loose ends are tied up before dinnertime is a Finisher. This is the person who makes sure all their tasks are completed before going to bed for the night. I personally fit into the "Early Riser" and "Finisher" spots, so if you are posting on social media trying to get a person like me to pay attention, and you are posting at 10 AM every day, I might not see you. I've got too much work to do during the day, even though I have Messenger open all day like it's my email! But bet your ass, I'm on the newsfeed the first and last thing every day. If you have never thought about the importance of time in your social media strategy, you need to start factoring it in.

Social media is becoming more and more intelligent on a daily basis. Arming yourself with information like this will make the difference between people who play on social media vs. people who get paid on social media.

Trust me on this, my clients and the people around the world just like them will take your clients if you are not careful. These are people who are investing their time and money into learning what it is going to take to market their business in the near future. I encourage you to take action as well.

Chapter 19:

How to Use Social Media to Close More Deals Without Being a Pushy Salesperson

C'mon folks, the days of being able to close on most sales transactions with the style of a pushy used car salesman, are gone. That window closed over a year ago. Now you must learn how to use social media to close more deals.

Not that you can't still close people, but the residual factor is usually gone when you use this approach. We now have to consider the "Life Time Value" (LTV) of each prospect we come across.

The reason is simply because of social media. Thanks to thought leaders like Mark Zuckerberg, the whole way that we perceive salespeople and marketing tactics, is changing at a rapid pace. Plus, now we have a way to stay connected and engaged with our clients/prospects in a seemingly real way. It's every salesperson's goal to be the first person past clients think of when they are ready to buy their product and services again. Thanks to social media you can make that happen. You just have to be cool about it.

Social is Visual

We are becoming more visually stimulated beings. We want to look at content with infographics. We want to look at Facebook posts with pictures. On a side note, I think it is all Pinterest's fault. Things that really stand out and are aesthetically pleasing to our eyes are the only things that matter these days. It's no longer a world where cold hard sales calls full of feature dumping, are the most effective way of marketing. Matter of fact they are the least effective.

Is Email Effective?

Let's talk about the variety of ways you can stay in touch with your past, present and future clients. First up, let's look at email. Email is no longer considered one of the most influential ways to market. The truth is, the average email open rate is only 12%. Don't EVEN allow me to go there on direct mail. Most of it gets thrown away, and only 7% of direct-mailers actually show a positive ROI. Even traditional media is becoming less and less influential (unless you're in politics). Only 16% of all TV and radio marketing campaigns yield a positive ROI. Now, don't get me wrong. If you are doing these things, you are good at them and getting above average results, DON'T STOP. Always keep doing what works.

Solve Problems Rather than "Selling"

What these numbers tell us, is that our audience is getting smarter. They're getting more hip to the same old sales pitches. The marketplace is demanding for someone to listen to them, someone to give them transparency in marketing, someone to show them where their pain actually is, and then cure that pain. You need to step into that space and step out of being an old-school pushy salesperson. You are now responsible for being THE expert consultant, with a much-needed solution to their big a$$ problem. It's at this point when your sphere of influence buys from you and that you become a "Closer," the sales equivalent of a "Made (Wo)Man." It's that plain and simple. So, you might ask "That's all fine and cool, but how do I go about doing that?" My answer to you is simple. "Follow the steps below."

1. Listen to Your Audience:

How do you listen to your audience without physically talking to them? The best way to listen to your audience, without having to pick up a phone and have a conversation with them, or without having to really get to know them better is to stalk them online. Take a look at their Facebook page. Take a look at their Twitter, their LinkedIn page; find out the things that they're saying. Actually read their posts. Look at their pictures and familiarize yourself with their online character. Chances are, what they care about on SM and in life are usually the same. See if your prospects talk about their family life. See if they are into sports. Look and see how often they post about teir business. This gives you instant ammo to start a conversation that they also WANT to have. With a little finesse, you will have them telling you what you need to hear to close the deal.

2. Connect and Engage with Your Audience:

We all know that it takes seven touches to influence an individual and for them to become familiar with you. We also know that people buy from people they know, like and trust. With these things in mind, the easiest, fastest, and most influential way to accomplish the seven touches you need can be done easily via social media.

The first touch comes from the prospect seeing your post.

The second touch comes from when they like or comment on your post.

The third touch comes from you @tagging them in your response comment.

The fourth touch is a gimme; everyone likes to see their name written and hear it spoken.

The fifth is when almost all SM sites automatically send an email when you mention them, retweet them or engage in some way.

The sixth and seventh are when you keep the conversation going by keeping the comments engaging.

Remember this: Statements end in a period. To really engage, your sentences should end in question marks. The sixth and seventh touches immediately cause influence and familiarity with your audience. This compels them to buy from you, without you having to jam features and verbally vomit why they should be buying from you. Let them come to you and say, "This is why I'm with you; it's because of your expertise."

3. Question the Confession:
So, what does "question the confession" actually mean? Well first off, that's my saying. I believe you have to ask the right questions to make a sale. Too often salespeople try to tell, tell, tell, tell, tell, tell, tell. If I'm constantly just telling you stuff/features, and even if you're listening, I'm only trying to convince you of what I'm not closing, A true closer is waiting for the prospect to talk about the bad. Many times, we are on sales calls and listening but only to the good things. Who cares about good things? If things were good, you would not

be talking. Poke around and ask the hard questions, the ones that make them uncomfortable and realize they need improvement. Then once they tell you what that pain is, tell them you can make that pain go away. Easy, simple and a lot fewer words and energy.

The Sales Conversation

But there's one more thing you must know. There's a big difference between a conversation and a SALES conversation. A conversation happens when you're talking to someone about your business, who has no inclination of buying your stuff and is not even remotely interested in your services. A sales conversation is knowing you have someone on the line who has the ability to buy your product. A sales conversation happens with someone who can significantly and immediately benefit from what you have. Now with that being clear…

Ask More Questions

If we are having a sales conversation, then what? Turn that conversation completely over to them. You ask short questions; they give long answers. If their answers are short, ask more/better questions. This requires a great deal of patience. In the end, they will have told you what they are good at, and if you are good, they will have told you what they are bad at. It's at that very moment you offer the solution you know will fix the problem. If they show resistance, your response is simply "But you did say that you (insert what they said here)." It is at that point they will usually say, "You're right, thank you. Let's do this" These are the three simple steps you can use to convert social media friends into great customers who you know and like working with. Try it. It is not easy, but it is simple. If you will just have a little patience and wait for them to tell it, you can SELL IT!

Chapter 20:

If You're on Social Media WHY Are You Not Being Social?

Allow me to give you the upfront, no-bullshit truth about social media. To understand what social media truly is, you must have a good understanding of the evolution of communication. Back in the 80s when cell phones first made their debut, people said things like "I'm only giving my cell phone number to friends and family." All of a sudden, people like me started stepping up and saying, "I'm here to do business. I'll give my cell phone number to anyone. My clients can contact me anytime. I provide service." The people who resisted at first were forced to follow suit and give their cell numbers out. The problem was they were running from behind instead of leading from ahead. In the 90s, the same type of action occurred. The invention of the email address forever changed the way we communicate. In the beginning, people said, "I don't want spam or strangers to have my email." Again, someone like me stepped up and said, "I'm going to put my email on every website I can. I want people to find me from all over the world." Those who resisted, in the beginning, were forced to relent. In 2008, people were saying, "I'm not going to learn texting. It's a fad. If someone wants me, they will call." Those same people probably felt stupid asking their friends how to text in 2010. This is no laughing matter here, folks... People have said the same thing about social media. They say, "My social media profiles are for my friends and family only. I don't want strangers to see what I do online." Here's the truth: Social Media is just another form of communication. It is no different from email, text, snail mail, phone calls, text, carrier pigeon, etc. Simply put, these are all forms of communication.

Different audiences communicate via different modalities. By far the most popular way to communicate online these days is Facebook. With over one billion users and the largest amount of Google juice on the planet, Facebook is where it's at. If you are keeping your Facebook profile and posts private, you need to OPEN UP. Most consumers start their search process online. Most consumers also cross-reference Google with who they are doing business with. This means your clients are probably Googling your name. They want to see if anything good or bad, is out there online with your name on it. They want to have a deeper sense of who they are trusting. Knowing that Facebook is generally the number one result that shows up when you search a person's name, it's important to have an open profile on Facebook. Let your audience get to know you. Let them see you for who you are. If you act a fool on Facebook, you probably don't deserve the business anyway. We have all heard the saying, "Your network is your net worth." Why would you think it would not apply to your "social network"? WAKE UP! The time is now, and the window is closing. You still have a chance to take control of your social media and get on the right track to attract the customers you want.

Chapter 21:

This B2B Strategy Gets You in Front of the Decision Maker Fast

In the B2B world, the single biggest struggle is getting past gatekeepers and in front of the decision maker. Gatekeepers are better than ever at their jobs. C-level executives are buried in secretaries, assistants, managers and PR executives. The good ones are the hardest to reach, too.

First, you must understand there are reasons decision makers aren't easily accessed. One of those reasons is to protect them from you, the salesperson. Decision makers get pitched everywhere they go and on every call they take.

This is distracting AF, and for them to keep focused on all the other stuff they must do, they have to hide from sales pitches.

Basically, you're playing the corporate equivalent of cops and robbers. You're trying to track down and capture business from someone who doesn't want to be captured. You're gonna need to go all forensic on them. You're gonna need some clues to make your case. The good news is, I got you, fam!

First, you can NEVER – EVER – EVER call and say something like, "Can I talk to the manager or hiring agent?" You better know exactly who you are contacting. You need to call and say, "Can I talk to Harold in HR?" Act like you know who you want to speak with and that you belong on the phone with them.

If you don't know the decision maker's name, you are just being lazy, and gatekeepers know it. These days we have Facebook, LinkedIn and Twitter. Not to mention the company website and roster.

The first step to getting in front of the decision maker is finding out WHO the decision maker is. You need to know their name and their title. Once you know who you're looking to pitch, you need to know HOW to pitch them. This is where the clue-finding forensics come in. It's time to go full-on stalker status. Creep all over their social media; send them connection requests and start fact-finding.

You're not looking into their job. You're looking into their personal life. People buy from people they like and know. You need to know what they like, so you can use it to leverage them to like you. Are they into sports? Reading books? Do they have any hobbies like CrossFit or golf? These are the things you're looking for.

You also need to learn who your common connections are, so you can hit those people up and ask what they know about the prospect. Then ask them if they can make an introduction for you. Leverage every single thing you can.

While other salespeople are trying to pitch a similar product as yours to the same prospect you are, you will stand out. Also, while they are fighting the gatekeeper, you'll be making moves. Abe Lincoln once said, "If I had five minutes to cut down a tree, I'd spend three of them sharpening my ax."

Research sharpens your ax for when you go in for the chop.

Once you figure out their hobbies, likes and lifestyle, you can work your magic. First, when you send a DM on LinkedIn, send them something they find interesting. If they are into spearfishing, go to YouTube, pull up the coolest spearfishing video you can find, send it to them and say something like:

"I know you're into spearfishing. I've been thinking about trying it out. I'm looking at going to Pensacola, Florida. Have you been there? I hear the grouper are a good start for rookie spearfishermen. Any thoughts?"

Notice there's nothing about work in there?

You see, work will come. But first, you have to show them you care about them. The fastest way to get someone's attention is to pay attention to them. When you show up talking about their hobby, you demonstrate you're paying attention. The whole reason people put stuff on social media is so others will pay attention to them. You're doing just that.

If they are into sports, talk about the latest game and invite them to a game with you. Don't be a cheap bastard either. You gotta spend money to make money. Plus, if you take a client to a sports game, strip club or bar, it's a write-off. You spent that money to acquire business. (Talk to your CPA. I have no clue.)

If you can't get them to respond on social media, or if they have a social media gatekeeper, you can use the mail. Send them something from Amazon. Send a business book from someone they like. Send a sports team jersey or bobblehead. Spend a few bucks and send them something that will make them want to call and thank you.

B2B sales aren't usually one-time closes. This a true corporate dating process. The good girls never let you bang on the first date. The good B2B accounts are the same way. If they jump into bed with you fast, they will do the same thing with your competitor if the opportunity arises.

Chapter 22:

5 Secrets to Generating Real Estate Listing Leads from Facebook Ads

No one just rolls over in the middle of the night and tells their spouse, "Let's pack all our shit in boxes and scream at each other for the next month." That's not why people list their homes. Selling a home for most is a major life event. It's the biggest windfall of money most people ever see. For others, it's the biggest loss.

You've got to also remember no one has ever logged into Facebook to find a real estate agent. That's just not why people get on The Book. They go on FB to see what their friends are doing and what's going on in the world.

Yet, the facts I just gave you are ignored daily by real estate agents running ads. I see ads every day from Realtors in my newsfeed. Ninety-nine percent of those ads have zero clicks, no likes and make the agent look like a fool.

Chances are since you're reading this, you may have had a few of your ads fail, too.

Over the last eight years, I've created over 1,500 Facebook ads. Over 400 of those ads were for real estate leads. I've spent a lot of time, money, effort and thought to get the best real estate leads possible from Facebook. Turns out, it's a helluva lot easier than most attempt to make it.

1. No One Wants a Realtor:
It amazes me, the narcissism some agents have. They put their pictures on signs, cards, logos and more but nobody on this planet wants a Realtor. What they want is their home sold. Most homeowners wouldn't give a shit if you were green with purple sprinkles as long as you sold their home. Realtors are simply the middlemen in between what the prospect has now and what they want.

The reason I tell you this is not to be mean but to let you know that advertising yourself as a Realtor is a terrible ad strategy on Facebook. Instead, you need to focus on selling homes. Your ads, fan page and funnel, should be based on neighborhoods and districts, not you, the agent. Run ads selling homes and you'll get more leads than if you ran ads selling an agent.

2. You Need an Offer:

Most ads I see agents running have terrible offers, too. They say things like "Let me list your home today," or "I sell homes in 30 days or less." Those offers are weak, and they play to the narcissistic agent, not the prospect. A good offer for a listing ad would be something like "Your Neighbor's House Just Sold Over List Price in Less Than 36 Hours. Find Out How." See the difference?

The curiosity from my offer draws them in; then when they realize what the other homes in the area are selling for, they consider getting an opinion from an agent on what they can sell their home for. If you want to get listing leads, build curiosity in the home, not familiarity in the agent.

·

3. Create a Sales Funnel:

These days, sales funnels are all the rage. I'm sure you see ads in your newsfeed 10 times a day saying they have the perfect funnel or they will build you the perfect funnel. Everyone and their momma want to sell stuff to Realtors because they know there are millions of you and they think you are easy to sell to. Beware of the people selling funnels. Sometimes, they can be a waste of cash.

My new company, PhoneSites makes it so easy and affordable to create funnels that a 12-year-old can do it. You're only being lazy and complacent if you don't learn to use idiot-proof software to generate a ton of listing leads.

4. Learn to Farm:
Farming still works, and it's easier and cheaper than ever before. Yet, so many agents are missing the mark and still sending out junk mail. You can use Facebook to target zip codes. Imagine putting your ad in front of an entire zip code daily for a month for a fraction of the price of one mailer. That's what FB farming is.
The key to generating leads is familiarity. Repetition creates familiarity. It's your job to repeatedly market to

the same zip code over and over again. You can always change offers, but you gotta STAY in front of the same people. Pick a territory to farm and don't stop running ads until your crops grow!

5. Follow-Up Is Key:

The chances of someone seeing an ad on Facebook, contacting you and listing their home in the same day are highly unlikely. Thus, the insatiable need for follow-up. You've got to have calls, texts and emails going out to the lead at least once a day for the first three days. This gives you nine touches to get a hold of them; eight is the number of familiarities usually, so nine contacts is one contact above and beyond.

You need to set up automation for the follow-up. Even if you only get five leads a week, you have to remember the average person needs 90 days to sell their home. That's 75 leads you're following up within just three months. If you don't have automation set-up, you will miss out on listings.

You should only be talking to leads when they are ready to make a move. The rest should be on autopilot.

Last year I personally ran ads for a luxury community in Austin, Texas called "Lakeside at Rough Hollow." The sales rep set an all-time record in the neighborhood from the leads I sent her. She's also a badass closer. I'm pretty sure she sold over $8 million in real estate directly from the leads I sent her. (I no longer do this for anyone but me.)

My client and friend, Adam Stark has used these secrets to become the number one agent in his entire market. He's literally gone from sleeping on a friend's couch to being the most known person in his city. Social media advertising allows him to list and sell more than anyone who competes against him.

Chapter 23:

What It Takes to Be a Savage on the Phone

Being "good on the phone" isn't the same as it used to be. Most people think phone skills revolve around smiling and dialing. Turns out, that's old-school thinking that won't serve you well long-term.

The way we use the phone has changed. It's time salespeople change with it.

Right now, 86% of all phone calls go unanswered. Yet 90% of text messages are read. Both of these actions take place on the phone. Which do you think is more efficient? My time and money are going on the 90% read rate versus the 14% answer rate.

Being good on the phone now includes your ability to send texts, DMs and emails. In my analytics accounts, across the board, I see that 80% of my traffic is mobile. I even stopped running ads to desktop computers months ago.

The phone is more than just a talking device.

We use our phones for everything, yet when it comes to work, we limit it to voice calls. People aren't into voice calls like they used to be. Caller ID, call blocking and online number searches keep a lot of salespeople from even getting an answer or a returned phone call.

To be effective at sales, you have to meet the prospects where they want to be sold. If they prefer to use text messages to communicate, close them via text. Trying to flip a prospect from text to voice is just another roadblock and objection that YOU create. Keep the conversation where it started unless the prospect asks otherwise.

To be a savage on the phone in modern times, you need more than the ability to talk. You need the ability to communicate.

Communication covers it all. Voice is only one way to communicate. Text, email and social media are also ways to communicate.

Selling via text takes patience. This is a good thing. It allows you to slow the sale down and choose your words wisely. Going back and reading paste text closes is like listening to your past sales calls. Grade yourself; get better. Most salespeople rush through voice sales. Text is the exact opposite. Slow, methodical and precise.

Let's don't forget about video. Most videos these days are made from handheld smartphones. There are even entire cinematic movies that have been shot from iPhones.

Video is the number one way to influence an audience.

All our lives we've grown up watching TV. Our parents told us "The people on TV are important." So, we've essentially been hypnotized by people on screens. You have a unique opportunity to leverage this deeply-rooted sublime programming to your advantage.

The number one fear in America is not snakes, bears, racist cops or even Trump; it's public speaking. Video is the ultimate public speaking platform.

When you get on video and demonstrate expertise, you become an almost instant authority.

A modern-day savage is a salesperson with phone communication skills, not just the traditional calling skills. People are harder and harder to reach via voice dial. Be smart. Follow the trend and use ALL the other functions of the phone to make sales. While your competitors are talking to one prospect at a time, you could be texting with eight and sending a video to thousands more.

Chapter 24:

The Number One Mistake Salespeople Are Making Online

For the life of me, I can't begin to understand why people behave the way they do online. Somewhere, along the lines, we've been programmed to behave differently online than we act in real life. From trolls to arguing politics, to bashing each other, these are normal things online, but not normal off.

I'm a firm believer in being the same way offline as you are online.

Especially when it comes to sales. Salespeople tend to think you have to sell differently from email, text, social media and through video than you do when you're face-to-face. I'm here to tell you; you don't! You need to sell exactly online, the way you sell offline. The formula is the same; the communication device is the only difference.

The salespeople who learn to master the online process in the same way they've mastered the face-to-face selling process will be the salespeople who survive as more and more "robots" replace jobs.

Chapter 25:

Can You Complete This 30-Day Sales Challenge?

The new year is the time of year when people join weight loss challenges, goal challenges and all that fun stuff. I've decided to get in on the action and create a 30-days sales challenge for you. With my sales challenger, you'll get the year started off with momentum on your side.

After all, those goals ain't gonna reach themselves.

I've been issuing this challenge to my mastermind clients since 2013. With over 3,000 people who've gone through the program, not a single f'n one has completed this challenge. Were they lazy? No! Was it too hard? No! The problem is they got too busy from doing the challenge, that they never had time to complete it. When you're closing sales, you have no time for anything else.

For the first time, outside of my mastermind program, I'm going to share with you, my 30-day sales challenge.

If you're up to the task, I'll help you fill your pipeline like a champ. If you do exactly as I'm about to tell you to do, in the next 30 days, you will be flooded with sales. No matter what it is you sell, just trust my process and do what I say.

The shit works as long as you work it.

I'm not going to tell you to make cold calls, knock doors, go to networking events or any of that archaic stuff. I'll show you how easy it can be to accumulate a pipeline and close sales while sitting on your ass in front of a computer.

I'm going to give you three things to do, every day, online, for 30 days. They will not be hard. They won't take much time, and you will get out of it what you put into it. As I've stated before, my clients who pay $2,500/month to work with me, struggle to complete this challenge due to the influx of leads they have in the first two weeks.

Each day, for the next 30 days, you'll repeat these actions. Each day, the exercise compounds and adds to your follow-up. The key to making the most sales from this strategy is going to be who you target not how many you target.

Before you begin the exercise, you must create a Dream 100 list. The Dream 100 comes from Chet Holmes and the book *The Ultimate Sales Machine*. "The Dream 100" concept is brilliant. You need to make a list of 100 dream clients, that you'd die to get business from or do business with. This is the first step of the challenge. For the challenge to work properly, you need to know who you're going after. Once you've got your list of 100 people, the clock starts, and the challenge begins. You'll note this strategy is similar to the Lucky 7 Method I mentioned earlier, but this challenge goes on for 100 prospects! Like I said, no one has been able to finish it!

Every day, for the next 30 days, you'll do the following three things. Whether it be on LinkedIn, Twitter, Facebook, Instagram or any other social media channel, you gotta do the work. The network you choose to use doesn't matter as long as it's the network where your Dream 100 are.

First, each day you will write on one of your Dream 100's walls. Go to their profile and leave them a message. Not just any message, though. An engaging message that lets them know you're paying attention. Before you just go crazy firing off random wall postings, read my article/watch my video on Strategic Selling with Social Reconnaissance on HardcoreCloser.com. Then find out what they like, have been doing and want to talk about.

Start the conversation with them on their wall.

The best way to get engagement and strike up a conversation would be to ask a question. "Hey man, I saw you went to the zoo last week. Looks fun! Did your kids like it? I'm thinking about taking my family." See what I did there? I drew them in with innocence. After we go back and forth, we create a bond of familiarity. The more they like and know me, the better chance I have to swoop in and close them on something.

Second, every day for 30 days, you need to send someone a DM. Not a dick pic either. I'm talking about doing the same type of thing as I explained above, on their wall, but to a different person's DM. Go to their wall, see what they are into, then send them a DM about it, to get the conversation started.

There's a natural progression of conversation. There's the friendly part, then the "how's family?" part and then "how's business?" part. It's when it shifts to "how's business?" that you say, "Business is good, but I'm always looking to help people like you or the folks you know. If you EVER need anything from me, I'm your guy. Meanwhile, is there anything I can do to help you with work?" This is a powerful, simple, effective closing strategy that leads to thought and decision on behalf of the prospect.

The third and last thing you have to do daily is comment on one of your Dream 100's posts. The same principles apply. Seek out their wall; see what they like, and comment on one of their posts with a question. Agreeing with them is always better than challenging them.
Agreeing with them and asking a question will engage them.

You can go on your Dream 100's timelines and select "see first" to make sure you don't miss any of their posts. This way, you have a selection of posts you see daily to prospect on. Oftentimes, you can engage them on their post and then flip them to the DM and further the "how's work?" conversation there.

After you've done this for 30 days straight, you'll have contacted 90 of your dream 100. You'll have started conversations and increased engagement with 90 people you would love to do business with. Surely, out of 90 people, 1-2 of them will decide they like you, want to work with you and give you their business.

Don't forget the follow-up. Strong relationships aren't built from one DM. They are built from familiarity and bonding. Follow up daily. Let them get to know, like and trust you before you go for the close.

Chapter 26:

9 Ways to Close Sales Using an Instagram Business Page

Instagram has made some pretty significant changes. They recently added a 10-second Snapchat video feature, which finally allows users to zoom in on pictures, but the biggest change is that they implemented business pages. Business pages change the game for those of us who use Instagram to promote our brands and products.

It's clear that Instagram is now on the same path Facebook has been on. The changes and the order of those changes are synonymous with Facebook's evolution. So, it makes total sense.

After all, Facebook owns Instagram.

Social media is not going anywhere anytime soon. It's no longer a fad. Especially Instagram. With over 800 million+ monthly users, it's safe to say Instagram is here for the long haul. I personally love the site. It's my favorite social media application. No politics, no spam (yet) and it's all user-generated. I spend a good amount of my online time searching hashtags on IG.

I've also used Instagram to make sales. You know me. I'm always closing! Instagram is no different. It took me a while to get down how it all works, but I've mastered IG selling at this point.

It's now another notch in my bedpost of places where I can go, and fuck shit up.

I'm the guy who's not gonna talk about something until I've done it and I feel qualified to talk about it, and I've now gained enough knowledge where I can share some of my expertise concerning selling on The Gram. Here's the deal, though, if you learn this stuff and don't do any of it, I guarantee you will not make any sales. You have to actually DO the stuff I'm about to share with you if you want to close sales on Instagram.

1. Use the Contact Button:

Since IG just added business pages, part of that entailed adding a "Contact" button on each business profile. This makes it easy for users, who are already on their phone to call or email you right from the Gram. The way to make sales is to get in contact with prospects. This feature makes it a snap to drive prospects to contact you when you promote the contact button in your posts. When you make a post, add a call to action at the end that says, "Let's talk. Contact us by tapping the button on our profile."

2. Track Insights:

Most of us in sales are not numbers people. We save that kind of work for guys like Harold over in HR. I'm just a guilty as the next person. Hell, I hire people to track numbers for me. The thing is, the numbers do help you to make more sales. Creating a post with a call to action is one thing. Creating a post with a call to action at the peak time your prospects are online is another entirely. Those who can sell by the numbers sell a lot.

3. Promote Posts:

Now that Facebook has tied in Instagram ads with ads manager, you can promote your posts from your business page. This now includes videos. Instagram has made it easy to promote them. Simply hit the "Promote" button on the post, then choose your audience and budget right from your phone. Remember this: If you're going to promote something, make sure you include a call to action.

4. Drive People to the DM:

I love the DM. I've made hundreds of thousands of dollars this year alone from DMs. When people send me a DM, I use a method called CATCH to allow me to close the vast majority of people who reach out. Knowing this, I invite people to DM me often. My profile description even says, "I respond to all DMs personally." The DM is where it all goes down.

5. Promote Your Profile:

You'll never make sales if no one has ever heard of you. We both know sales is a numbers game. It's a matter of how many people you can get in front of and how fast you can do it, too. Paying to promote your profile and then providing calls to action will help drive sales right where you want 'em. To you!

6. Reply to Comments:

It amazes me how many people ignore Instagram comments. I've made thousands of dollars just replying to comments on my pictures and videos. Instagram also makes it easy for you to send those people a DM. That's how I do it. I reply to a few comments publicly, but I also send DMs to many of my commenters. I told you, I've made a ton of cash using DMs, so that's where I want prospects to show up. Start the conversation on the post and close the conversation in the DM.

7. Thank People for Liking Your Pictures:

When people go out of their way to tap one of your pics, you should thank them. This allows you to get in front of them, shake their hand (digitally) and start the bond building you need to establish to ask for their business. The other bonus of replying, liking and sending DMs to people is that it keeps your pics in their newsfeed. Instagram made their newsfeed similar to Facebook, so you're not seeing posts in real time anymore; you need to engage to be seen.

8. Shoot at Least One Video Per Week:
You can now record up to 60 seconds of video at a time on Instagram. That's 50 seconds of value and 10 seconds of sales pitch and call to action if you know how to do it right. Videos on Instagram get priority in the newsfeed, so you need to take advantage often. People love videos and the shorter, the better. You can record a sales pitch once, and it will be seen by 30% of your followers. That's not even counting hashtag traffic.

9. Capture 5-10 Stories Per Week:
Not too long ago, Instagram released stories. This is a 10-second live capture feature similar to Snapchat. You'd be surprised what you can say in 10 seconds. People are all over Instagram stories, too. My stories get watched thousands of times. You can't skip out on stories. You should be doing one or more every day.

I fully believe in using every angle I can to get in front of more people who might benefit from my help. When it comes to making sales on Instagram, there's no exception. I'm selling in pictures, videos, comments, DMs, stories and every other method I can come up with.

Chapter 27:
The Ultimate Sales Follow-Up System

Do you even follow-up, bro? I've said it a million times, and I'll say it again, "The money is in the follow-up." The numbers don't lie. Most salespeople don't follow up. Yet the average prospect needs to be contacted 8-12 times to feel comfortable buying. Most sales aren't closed on the first call. If you're relying on one-call-closes only, you're missing out on a lot of cash.

.

Instead of a one call close, the goal should be to get through those 8-12 touches as fast as you can. Follow up or fall off. To close the sale, you must create familiarity and trust with the prospect. Rarely do we trust someone as soon as we meet them. We get to know someone before we decide if we trust them or not. How do you get to know someone? You communicate with them more than once. Simple.

Let me tell you a story of two salesmen.

I know this salesman. We will call him "Jon." Jon pays for new leads every single day. Each day, when he gets to his office, he knows he will have new leads, in his inbox, ready for him to call. Every day, he goes into work and contacts these leads. Jon closes around 20% of the leads he reaches on a daily basis. Since he has new leads each day, he only calls the leads once. If they close, they close. If not, he simply moves on to another new lead.

I know another salesman. We will call him "Ron." Ron bought a list of leads about six months ago. Just one leads list. One time. Every day Ron goes into work and calls the same leads over and over. It takes Ron about 60 days to ramp up, but he closes over 70% of his leads. He never gives up. He's a real buy or die guy.

Ron closes 50% more of his leads than Jon. Better yet, Ron bought one leads list, one time. Jon is buying new leads every day. Ron not only has a higher conversion percentage; he has a lower lead cost, too.

The sale is in the follow-up.
Often, salespeople are afraid to follow up. They offer zero value, make hard-to-believe claims, then move on and abandon the prospect, leaving them to find a

solution to their problem, on their own. Not cool dammit! NOT COOL! Humans are indecisive by nature. If you offer the solution to their problem, you owe it to them to follow up with them until they let you solve it. If not, you're lazy and greedy. Plain and simple.

I'm gonna help you out today. I'm going to give you a follow-up system that's easy to implement, costs you nothing and will help you close more sales. Here's the thing, though, this ain't my first rodeo. I know this chapter is 100% free, therefore of little value to you. The words in this chapter, however, have cost me millions of dollars to organize. The information is here; it's up to you to take action on it. **Don't discount the simplicity**.

After you've made initial contact and the prospect is not convinced to buy what you sell, instead of pressuring all you can and attempting to bully your way to a sale, sell the follow-up. That's right. If you know they aren't ready to buy; then it's time to sell the follow-up. At some point, they ARE going to buy. You need to make sure you are the one they buy from.

Sell the follow-up.

You see, what happens a lot, is salespeople get off the phone, or leave the sales conversation feeling like an asshole. They feel guilty for putting a lot of pressure on the prospect and maybe even saying some shit they regret. Leaving it all on the field causes follow-up reluctance. The salesperson knows the prospect doesn't want to talk to them, so they refuse to follow up.

Instead, when you sell the follow-up, the prospect expects you to contact and continue selling them. If it's going to take 8-12 touches to create familiarity and trust, the salesperson needs to deliver enough value to earn the right to contact the prospect 8-12 times.

I earn the right to follow-up by asking. I ask if it's okay for me to email them. I ask them to follow me on social media. I ask if it's okay if I call them at a specific time and follow-up. I ask for the follow-up like I ask for the sale. I look at the 8-12 touches as trial closes that each get me one step closer to the "YES" I'm looking for.

It really is that simple. When you ask for the business and don't close the sale, ask for the follow-up. Then keep following up until you no longer have to.

Chapter 28:

10 Ways to Get Leads from LinkedIn

I recently got kicked off of Facebook. We had a situation where someone in our Sales Talk group was calling people's bosses and complaining about what they said in the group. This occurrence made me livid. Who does that shit?

Anyway, I went on a rant and posted in the group. I said some shit that goes against Facebook's policy and they gave me a 30-day ban.

Truth is, FB did me a favor. I needed a break. But that's a whole other story.

Since I've been off Facebook, I've made the transition to LinkedIn. I mean, I've always been on LinkedIn. I check it once or twice a week. This time, I got serious. I told myself I was going to get to know LinkedIn and make some sales from it. That's exactly what I did.

In three weeks, I made $30,000 in sales from DMs on LinkedIn. These sales come from people joining my programs. Turns out, the average user on LinkedIn earns $100K or more a year. It's a literal kangaroo-free zone. When people show interest there, they have the means and mean business about it.

I thought I'd share the ways I've made sales from LinkedIn, so you can do the same. These may seem too easy, but the easiest shit is always what sells the most. Remember that. Here's how you can get free leads from LinkedIn using some finesse and earning sweat equity.

1. Recommendations:
This is my favorite way to engage someone on LinkedIn. Start with flattery. First off, you need to mean what you say, but aside from that, flattery gets you a long way. I leave recommendations for my top 100 prospects. These recommendations also show up when people look at their profiles. I get double exposure, a chance to talk with the prospect and everyone wins.

2. Articles:

Each week, I publish two articles on LinkedIn. I just copy and paste existing articles from HardcoreCloser.com. If you don't have a blog, congratulations; LinkedIn is now your blog! It's free, and you can share articles you write anywhere. You can even add lead traps into your article, so you can use them for lead gen.

3. Groups:

Have you ever noticed how groups on LinkedIn email the shit out of you? I mean, you can swim to the middle of an ocean, get to a deserted island without a computer, and an email from a LinkedIn group will still come to you somehow. Look, if you can't beat 'em, join 'em. Use this spamming feature to your advantage. Just don't abuse it.

4. Posting Content:

Find articles you like from sites like *Entrepreneur, Inc.*, *Success, Forbes* and the usual suspects. Only when you post the content, ask for commentary. So many people forget that statements end with periods;

questions go on forever. Post viral content and ask for people to chime in. Engage them accordingly.

5. Sending DMs:
I'm a big fan of connecting with people and sending them DMs. Especially since on LinkedIn you don't really see people post too much. That's because, on LinkedIn, it goes down in the DM. Seriously, having a professional, behind-the-scenes DM chat is a powerful way to close a prospect. Especially if you use my CATCH method.

6. Commenting on Posts:
LinkedIn is the land of the silent. Hardly anyone engages on there. And when they do, they get emails and notifications out the ass. This leaves a wide-open opportunity for someone like you. You get their attention, engage them and then most likely you'll show up in their inbox. They will see you so much; they'll think they know you.

7. Sharing Posts:
If one of your prospects posts something useful or even something self-gratifying about themselves, you can

share it and get their attention. If they were featured in the news and they post the link, you can share it and congratulate them. People eat that shit up. It's a way to get cool points and strike up a relationship.

8. Commenting on Articles:

Once you comment on a popular article, your comment is there forever. Most people post an article and don't ever check comments. Meanwhile, if you're a sales beast and not a sales bitch, you'll go in and strike up conversations with people who've commented and turn them into connections.

9. Searching Hashtags:

Hashtags are used on LinkedIn, and most people overlook them. Yet, they are full of gold. Mostly old gold, but gold nonetheless. You can connect with other people who've shared the same hashtag as well as get your content found more easily by using common hashtags in your posts.

10. Emails:

Like I said earlier, LinkedIn is a fiend with emails. No matter what you do, you can't escape them. Group updates. Notifications. Daily recaps. Fucking LinkedIn will email the shit out of you, even when you tell it not to. That being said, you can use it to your advantage. Think about the actions that would cause LinkedIn to send emails and do them. Participate in conversations in groups; share posts; comment on popular content. The Link loves to email.

Chapter 29:
The Golden Rule of Growing Your LinkedIn Network

LinkedIn is a different type of social media platform. The implied feeling that your boss is watching you, tied together with the fact that LinkedIn is a recruiting haven, keeps people from being too social on LinkedIn. That shouldn't keep you from growing your LinkedIn network because it is important.

What goes down behind the scenes is a completely different story. LinkedIn offers segments (groups) that are like pockets of the office where you can hide from your boss and actually talk about what YOU LIKE. With that being said, LinkedIn is a behind-the-scenes social network. People do not "like" statuses and comment very often due to the insecurity of being fired.

What people do DO on LinkedIn is send direct messages and connect with people from within their groups. Don't get me wrong; people read the LinkedIn newsfeed; they just don't participate in socializing very often.

You still need to keep a constant status update flow on LinkedIn and at least once a week log in and grow your network. Many times, people have asked me "Ryan, how do I gain more influence on LinkedIn?" And my answer is simple.

The bottom line: *Become influential*.

So, how do you become influential?

First, you need to start creating influence. The easiest and fastest way to do this is to start giving recommendations of people you have done business with in the past and are connected to. I put a video on HardcoreCloser.com that covers exactly how to do just that.

Second, you need to invite your business email database to connect with you on LinkedIn. You can do this directly from LinkedIn, or you can copy your profile link, and write an email with the link pasted in. Either way, you need to get the people you already know, to connect with you there.

Third, once those people connect with you, then you can start writing recommendations and talking publicly about your past experiences with them. When you do this, you've created the Law of Reciprocity in its purest form.

If you start becoming a person influencing recommendations, endorsing businesses and talking about experiences with others in the past, you will find those same people will start talking about you (in most cases).

Chapter 30:

Sales Hack: Overcoming Prospect Objections Within Your Sales Pitch

When most people hear the word "pitch," they imagine someone robbing their time, not letting them go and suffering through listening to someone who won't STFU. Sadly, most salespeople blow sales pitches worse than Chipotle makes you blow up a toilet.

A sales pitch is not a one-way conversation.

Salespeople have this false illusion that a pitch is all them talking. The problem with this approach is that the prospect is aware of when they are being pitched. If it feels like a pitch, and they aren't ready to hear it, it will go in one ear and out the other. When you finally get the ear of a good prospect, the last thing you want them to do is ignore you.

If you're going to pitch someone, it better not just be for the sake of pitching. It should be for the sake of closing a sale. That's the intention of this chapter as well. While you might find some of the instructions which are to follow very simple, don't knock the power of the secret that's about to be shared with you.

I don't know how long you've been in sales, but if you've been in for at least a year, you know the usual objections the client dishes out. I call these "universal objections." These are the objections that will always apply no matter what you sell. Regardless of your price/product, you'll always hear them.

The objections you get that aren't universal and are specific to your product/service are called "situational objections." These are the objections that vary from job to job. They are unique to the niche you serve, but they come up from your prospects often.

Take the time to do the ultimate objection handling exercise and write down all the universal and situational objections you can think of. List them all out. Every single one.

Universal Objections:

-No money

-Talk to the partner/spouse

-Shop around

-Time crunch

Situational Objections:

-Specific to your product

-Wants the mechanics

-Is well-educated on your product

-Is unique to the industry you serve

After you've listed them all off, write a number next to them in the order in which they come up the most. In other words, if you ALWAYS get the money objection, put #1 next to it, and if you never hear them mention a spouse/partner put #10+ next to it. Count the number of objections, then number them (#1 being the most frequent and so on).

Let me give you an example. I'll explain and work it into my own sales pitch, so you can see the process unfold. For instance, I still get the money objection even though my mastermind is only $5K. I'll list out some of the objections I hear all the time.

My Top 5 Objections:

-I can't afford it

-I don't have the time

-It won't work for my industry

-I don't have any tech skills

-I need to ask my boss to pay for it

Now that I have some of my objections written out, (you need to list ALL yours; I used my top five to save us both time), I need to create a scripted conversation that works these objections and their rebuttals into the conversation casually. Remember, the best salespeople don't seem like they are selling you.

Chapter 31:
It's Your Civic Duty to Close Your
Prospects—Here's Why

One of the hardest things to get a human being to do is to make a decision. Don't believe me? Go home and ask your spouse what they want for dinner. Most of us can't even make up our mind on what we want to eat, which is crucial to our survival, so how can you expect a prospect to be decisive about spending their hard-earned money?

You see, decisions come with consequences and most humans have made horrible decisions in their lives and suffered bad consequences. To keep that from happening again, their subconscious kicks in and "protects" them from making a decision and possibly suffering from the consequences of their choice.

You owe it to your prospects to close them!

There's only one thing on this planet that we can't get more of. TIME!

You can always get more money.

You can always find more love.

You can always find another job.

You will never get more time.

Your prospects will spend their precious time resource shopping around for a "deal" or looking to make the "right decision," and they won't realize they are losing the only thing they can't get back. They can always go buy another whatever it is you sell, but they will never get THIS moment back.

Plus, let's be real. Most of us sell something that helps the prospect.

None of us are here to rip people off and hurt them. If you are that way, please fuck off and leave now. This industry ain't for you. We help people, and when we close them, we save them time. Therefore, we give them a better life. Even if we are more expensive, we don't save them money, but we save them time, and the richest people on Earth will tell you "Time is money."

When your prospects inform you they are shopping around, ask them why and how long they plan on spending their precious time to save a few bucks. If they spend 15 hours looking to save $1,000, but they could have made $2,000 working after they'd made a smart decision to buy from you, they are wasting money!

You owe it to your prospects to close them. It's not about the money. It's not about the product. It's about the time and decision to save time and handle business. Ask. Listen. Gain empathy. Confidently offer a solution (your product) and get your prospect to decide. Sales doesn't have to be complicated. The more you complicate things, the less likely you are to help people to decide. People don't like complicated decisions. Remember to practice Keeping It Simple Sales (KISS).

Chapter 32:

5 Go-To Text Replies That Close Sales

Even though I didn't write this post, I had to include it since the author of it, Arielle Elizabeth, dropped some major knowledge bombs about closing via text. Thanks, Arielle. You nailed it!

McDonald's founder, Ray Kroc, once said, "The definition of salesmanship is the gentle art of letting your customer have it your way." Despite how much time has passed since Ray described our profession so eloquently, it still holds true.

We question; we persuade, and we close, gently, until our prospects have it our way. Sales is sales—it always has been and will continue to be.

But the methods we use to sell, on the other hand, have seen more change than the water fountain at the mall where a rookie salesman blows his commission. Most notably, texting is slowly replacing phone calls, and it's time to hop on board.

Unless you sound like Morgan Freeman, no one cares if they hear your voice. Hang up the phone, text your leads, and close them with these five replies:

1. Doubtful Prospects:

"Men lie, women lie, numbers don't lie." In case you don't get Lil Wayne's lyrics, your prospect is doubting what you can do for them. It's annoying, isn't it? They have seen the numbers right there in front of them, but they're still acting like you're full of more crap than a diaper pail in a newborn's room.

They may even be telling you, "Yeah, but Hugh Jass down the street said I can do better." Okay, but Hugh Jass could be lying, the numbers ain't. Why? Because Jay-Z said…

2. Cost Vs. Value:

"A Mercedes has a higher upfront cost but comes with premium support and quality. That 1992 rust bucket will cost you less at first until it breaks down on the freeway and the only support you have is a bottle of Tylenol in the glovebox."

Your prospect isn't grasping cost versus value. How many times have you dealt with someone who thinks the cheaper option is the better option? Put it in terms anyone can understand and hammer home the real value behind paying more—what you get down the road.

3. **Your Prospect Can't See the Future**:
"You can plan a pretty picnic, but you can't predict the weather."

Simply put, you don't know what could happen tomorrow. Your prospect isn't considering the long term.

Somewhere there is a 54-year-old, father of three who doesn't think he needs the life insurance plan you're selling because he eats right, exercises and is super healthy. Let him know that he might be sitting on a checkered blanket, having fun in the sun now, but what happens if it starts pouring? He would rather his loved ones be shielded from the storm than huddled under a tree, wouldn't he?

And, yes, this is borrowed from Outkast.

4. People Fear Change:
If Henry Ford shrugged and said, "Well, we've always done it this way," there would still be horse-drawn carriages rollin' down 95.

Is your prospect being complacent and resisting change? Probably, because that's what humans do. As salespeople, we're a different breed. While we understand and embrace the adapt or die lifestyle, most don't.

Feel free to replace "95" with whatever well-known roadway exists near you—the point remains. Unless your prospect secretly enjoys scooping up horse poop, they will appreciate you relating how change can benefit society, and more importantly, them.

5. Understanding Details:
The details make the difference. Disneyland and an airport look the same at first glance. Both have long lines, security checks, and marked up concessions, but one only promises good times.

"All Realtors do one thing—sell houses." This is something that was really said to a friend of mine, and the person who said it couldn't be more wrong.

At face value, a lot of things look the same. LCD vs. plasma. Chocolate chip vs. oatmeal raisin cookies. Coke vs. Pepsi. Rice pudding vs. tapioca pudding; and like the proof that's in it, the differences are in the details.

Remind your prospect that Disneyland and LAX share a lot of similarities, too. Although, once you look closer, one will take you to the happiest place on earth; the other will have you flying in a tin can, with some woman named Brenda reclined into your knees, and the chance you'll be manhandled by a certain airline.

The point is...

The odds are you text your mom, your friends, or the random you met at a bar last week, daily. Put all that practice into play, start texting your leads and get to closing.

Chapter 33:
How to Murder Sales Quotas Without Working Yourself to Death

The only people who deny having quotas are cops. Other than that, we all (especially salespeople), have quotas to meet. The problem with sales quotas is that they can be set very high and bring a lot of stress and pressure into our lives.

In 2007, my roommate was a chick. She had this boyfriend who worked for UPS. One night, he told me why he was never going to get a raise at work. He said his job had a daily delivery quota to reach. The quota was insane and almost unattainable. Once you finally got good enough to hit the daily quota, it was raised. He knew the better he got at his job, the more work he would have to do, for the same pay.

I feel like many salespeople think like UPS. The more sales they make, the more time they have to spend at work, away from the things they really want to be doing. It's like the saying coined by the great philosopher Puff Daddy, "Mo money. Mo problems."

But it doesn't have to be that way.

We live in a time where you can have technology do the tedious work you begrudge on a daily basis.

You know, the shit most of us hate to do. Like follow-up, for example. We know it takes 8-12 touches in order to close most sales. Most salespeople think this means calling and emailing only 8-12 times.

Most of the 8-12 calls and emails you'll send will be the same thing. Matter of fact, over 90% of the calls you make will go directly to voicemail. So, why not automate your emails and voicemails? You can set up campaigns from AWeber and Slybroadcast to email and leave voicemails every other day for two weeks or so.

This makes it so you ONLY have to speak with people ready to buy what you sell. Think of how much time this saves you as a salesperson. Even more so, think of all the extra sales you'll close by actually following up with people.

It's truly a win-win situation for everyone.

Imagine your life with the proper systems in place. One we can use to resolve the main problem we face in sales: The fact that we spend most of our time doing things other than closing. Following up is not closing. Lead gen is not closing. The only time we get paid is when we close. So, why not only focus on closing and outsource everything else?

My best guess is that most salespeople don't realize how cheap it is to set all this up and how easy it is to implement. If everyone knew, then everyone would be doing it. Yet here we are, with all this technology, and most people are still spending hours each day manually calling and emailing prospects.

Think of what you could do with all the extra sales and the extra time. If you spend 10% of your day closing now, you'll spend 90% of your day doing something other than the tedious work you regret having to do daily.

With more follow-up going on, you'll undoubtedly get more sales in the door. This allows you to spend 20% of your time closing and 80% of your time on strategy. If you focus correctly, you'll use strategies on follow-up to convert higher numbers, and you'll use automation in other areas of your pipeline.

There's really no excuse for you to do things that don't pay you immediately.

I personally use a combination of touches to speed up the prospecting process on autopilot. I have a program that allows me to send DMs to people on Facebook on autopilot. I send three messages over the course of three days. On top of that, I send 1-2 emails per day to build rapport. Finally, I use Slybroadcast to send voicemails over the course of a few days. Occasionally, I'll send out mass texts, too. But only when it's the right fit. I don't like blowing up people's texts (at first).

The beauty of automation is that it's a one-and-done situation. On your normal day, you spend 10 hours doing the work. But if you spend 10 hours doing automation work, it's done forever. This is called "getting leverage," and so many salespeople miss the mark on it.

-You write 8 emails, and you're done for life.
-You record 8 voicemails, and you're done for life.
-You create 8 auto texts, and you're done for life.

How long can it take you to do all of the above? A day? A week? Would you be willing to put in a couple of months of work behind the scenes to make your life easier and your bank account fatter? You should be, if not, you ain't living right.

Chapter 34:

How to Still Close When the Prospect Tries to Cancel Via Text

You've been at the office all day. Smilin', dialin' and setting an appointment with anyone who'll set one with you. Finally, you get someone on the hook. They say they are coming to your office about 15 minutes before you close shop. It's about 20 minutes until closing time now. You get a text. You look down at your phone. The appointment canceled. SONOFABISH.

The only thing worse is when the prospect texts you saying they've changed their mind and need to cancel the order.

These days, thanks to text and email, breaking up is no longer hard to do. Text and email remove the emotion out of the process for many prospects. But what can you do? How do you deal with clients who cancel and break up with you via text?

CANCELLATIONS VIA TEXT ARE JUST TYPICAL OBJECTIONS IN DIGITAL FORM.

I've written articles about this before, but you must treat text messages the same way you treat face-to-face objections. You handle them and press forward.

If you were selling face-to-face, you'd remove the emotion, increase the perceived value and handle the objections. Text cancellations are no different. A text cancellation is just the prospect's way of avoiding a good decision. As we've discussed, most people are scared to death to make a good decision. Chances are, your prospect is no exception.

First, let's think of some common reasons prospects cancel appointments and back out of deals:

-Not enough time
-Price too high
-Spouse/partner not on board
-Found a better deal
-No longer need the product
Take the time to make your list of reasons. List them all. I just named five common objections in less than 30 seconds. You should list about 20-30 reasons they

might cancel and flake out on you. Once you get these reasons written down, write the solution next to them.

For Example:
–Not enough time —> Bring product to them
–Price too high —> Increase perceived value
–Spouse/partner not on board —> Offer to speak with them
–Found a better deal —> Offer to match and bonus
–No longer need the product —> Re-sell or ask for referrals

Once you finish this exercise, you can move on to the next step. Remember, you should have 20-30 objections and 20-30 comebacks. Study these every day for 60 days, and you'll be a stone-cold closing machine. If you want to get real freaky with it, add the most common comebacks to your "text replacement" in your phone. I do this, and it saves me so much time.
Okay, so now that you're prepared for the objections and cancellations, it's time to change their mind. Remember, face-to-face and text-to-text are no different. The same universal laws of communication

exist. This means you have to remove ego and emotion to press forward.

The AFS (average frustrated salesman) either ignores the text, tries to call (no) or takes it personally and lashes back out at the prospect. None of these options work. You can't call someone who canceled via text. They are obviously uncomfortable and don't want to talk. You've got to use persuasive sales skills via text.

Most salespeople don't know this, but one of the main keys to closing is simply asking a second time. No shit, it really works. When the prospect's "no" isn't as strong as your "yes," they tend to fold and conform to purchasing. Simply asking a second time can make all the difference in the world. A simple reply with "I'm sorry you don't have time to come by today. I'd like to come to you. Where can we meet?" can make the difference in no sales and mo' sales.

Still, the prospect feels safe via text, and they usually have really poor text skills. Modern salespeople need to be just as good at selling via text as they are at selling on the phone or face-to-face. While others work on being good on the phone, the phone is dying.

If you have superior texting skills, you'll be equally as persuasive via text as you are in person. Sure, they can ignore you and not text back, but if you hit them with the right words and questions, you'll lure them right back to you.

The true key is mindset. Your mindset needs to be that text cancellations are no different than face-to-face objections. Your job as a sales pro is to handle and overcome these objections. As we evolve, more and more conversations are going to be had on text and not in person. Embrace it, get good at texting and man up.

Chapter 35:

3 Steps to Quickly Breaking a Sales Slump

Rock bottom? Yeah. I've been there a few times. Which is a few more than I'd like, but it is what it is, and it's in the past. I've suffered slumps that I thought would never end. Missing a few sales is one thing. Missing a few sales and being a month from going to federal prison is next-level slump shit.

The year was 2007. On April 15th I was sentenced to 15 months fed time. I had 60 days to sell all I could to prepare myself for a little over a year of incarceration. Needless to say, my mind was not on selling mortgages. Up until April 15th, I had been really distracted and couldn't seem to get out of it.

On April 15th, when the judge gave me my time, I had to shake my slump, get serious as fuck and get my life together for the next two months.

Sadly, this wasn't the first or the last time I'd have to perform under intense pressure.

Prior to April 15th, I had been in a slump. I had been dragging my ass, sleeping in later and feeling sorry for myself. You know, the trifecta of fucking up. When the judge slammed the gavel, I had to wake up, snap out of it and start kicking ass immediately. In retrospect, there were three things I did that allowed me to make $100K in less than 60 days back in 2007.

You may be faced with spousal infidelity, divorce, child issues, insane bills or whatever. No matter what you're facing, be glad you're free and able to face it. The pressure you're under was created by you and you alone. Just like I caused the issue that sent me to prison, you caused the issue that got you where you are. The sooner you own it, the sooner you can get over it.

In 2014, I was served with divorce papers and kicked out of my home. My wife, at the time, was awarded the home and I had to make a move. My bank account was frozen, and I had to spend my last dollars on a stupid-ass lawyer. I also needed $10K quickly to move to a new place. I had to snap from my slump again and get over it.

Here's how I did it in three steps.

1. Get Focused on the Solution:
First, you must find out what it is that you need/want to happen. Identify what I call the "trigger." The trigger is the thing that needs to happen to make everything get back to normal. The trigger is not making more money. The trigger is what you plan to do with the money to make what needs to happen, happen.

Once you identify the trigger, you need to obsess over it. I'm talking relentless obsession. If you put all of your time, focus and attention on the trigger, your mind will be too busy to remember that it's in a slump. You get what you obsess over. You might as well obsess over solutions instead of your problem.

2. Change Your Routine:
You can't get something new by doing the same old shit. If you want different results, you have to try different shit. The routine you're in during the slump is the routine that got you there. You gotta break that shit. Life comes in patterns. We are creatures of habit. You need to switch up your habits and routine.

For example, if you make calls in the morning, switch to the afternoon. If you send emails with the same old lines in them, write new ones. You must change if you want to see change. If you work from home now, you need to move to Starbucks or a friend's office. You've got to switch it up. This sends signals to the brain that help break slumps, too.

3. Find a Slump-Buster:

A slump-buster is a laydown sale that helps you break the losing streak. It's a professional baseball term used by upstanding guys like José Canseco. When MLB players have a no-hit streak, they go bang a big girl to break their patterns up. The big girls are called "slump-busters." In sales, a slump-buster is a laydown sale that you know you can close.

It's the confidence builder that reminds you, you still have it and can go on to dominate. You get a slump-buster sale under your belt, and you're one step closer to the trigger. Double points when the slump-buster is the trigger!

It's inevitable that life is going to pressure you into a slump from time to time.

Sales is a numbers game. It's a gamble. Sometimes you're hot; sometimes you're not. When you get on a hot streak, remember what you did and use it as leverage down the road when you go cold.

Chapter 36:

5 Skills That Will Be Mandatory in the Near Future for Salespeople

Unless you're stuck making B2B cold calls for IBM, you've noticed the sales landscape is changing at a rapid pace. The old-school salesman who's good on the phone is fading faster than Blockbuster Video. There's a new wave of sales skills in demand, and before long they will be mandatory.

Businesses are doing their best to move away from the typical salesman and to the salesman of the future. It's all a part of evolution. For years now, companies have treated the word "salesman" like the plague. They have avoided using it as much as they can. Instead, titles like "customer service rep," "satisfaction department," and other code names for "salesman" are put in place to make the prospects feel safe from the big bad salesman out there.

The shift is happening. I see it every day. The top salespeople on the planet are no longer the sharp-dressed, fast-talking, Rolex-wearing, Wall Street-type.

Instead, they are tech-savvy geniuses who know how to extract prospects from any niche.

Recently, I was at a hedge fund office. Everyone in the office, including salespeople, were dressed casually. The salespeople at this billion-dollar hedge fund, sold via technology and the web. Not face-to-face or on the phone.

They collect millions on autopilot. This is not only the future of sales; it's the present.

I've made a list of five skills that are going to be mandatory for salespeople to possess in the near future. If you're not already practicing and mastering these skills, you should be. Everything about this planet and the human race depends on evolution. If you don't evolve with it, you will go the way of the saber-toothed tiger.

1. Persuasive Writing:
Most salespeople think their skill lies with the phone or face-to-face sales. In modern times, the phone is rarely answered. This means the majority of the time the

phone is useless. If you're solely relying on your phone skills, you'll soon be left behind.

Instead, you need to learn how to write. You need to learn to text, email and write sales copy ASAP! The world is morphing from people who love to talk, into people who love to read. The signs are there. Don't make the mistake of avoiding them. If you want to get better at writing, look up John Carlton, Ben Settle and Harlan Kilstein.

2. Sales Funnel Design:

This skill is fairly new to the sales community and it's not to be avoided. In case you don't know, a sales funnel is a series of websites designed to capture consumer information and sell them your product. They are surprisingly easy to create, yet most salespeople ignore them as if they will simply go away.

To build sales funnels, you need to learn how to use my new software, PhoneSites. These technologies are drag and drop, point and click and paired with the right words; they will collect leads and fill your sales pipeline

24/7. They are cheap, easy to use and waiting for you to step up and learn them.

3. List Building:

Let me share a scenario with you. Dunstan is 23 years old. He's a computer wiz and has funnels which generate leads daily for him. He's been building this list of leads for over two years while in college. George is 55 and is a beast on the phone. He has no database or list of prospects, but if you put him on the phone, he can close. Who do you think will get hired on the job first? Dunstan with a list of hundreds of hit prospects or George, who has no prospects but can work the phone? If you said George you're wrong.

Today, companies care about data more than anything else. The more data and information you have on people, the more usable it is for companies to profit from. If you have list-building skills, you'll go a long way in sales with companies in the future.

4. Internet Marketing:

The internet is here to say. It's only getting more powerful. We are making a shift from staring at computer screens to staring through virtual reality glasses. The internet shows ZERO signs of slowing down or regressing. Companies know the internet is an endless pool of prospects all in one place. Because of this, they look for salespeople who can leverage it.

Internet marketing is not the way of the future. It's the current way. Matter of fact, it's been the biggest source of leads and sales on the planet since 2009. More digital ads are bought each year than traditional ones. Companies like P&G spend billions in online marketing annually.

5. Online Networking:
The new networking is social networking. Companies are looking for salespeople who can build, work and close their own sphere of influence, without having to travel all over and buy dinner and drinks on the company credit card. If you can log in to Facebook, engage a few users and lead them to a sale, you're about as powerful a salesman as they come.

You need to focus on the art of networking online if you want to have a successful sales career in the near future.

Chapter 37:

Why You Need to Immediately Stop Trying to Sell to Everyone

I'm about to drop some truth bombs on you that some of you ain't trying to hear. It's okay; I used to think the old-school way, too. Problem is, old-school thinking won't get you far in the modern marketplace. I'm about to teach you a sales secret that if applied, will lead you down the path to massive success selling anything to anyone.

Not everyone is a prospect for you.

A lot of salespeople spend too much time trying to close the wrong people. This takes away time they could spend selling to the right people. Most of us are hard heads, though. We spend our time trying to close prospects we shouldn't have even been talking to in the first place. Then, when we catch a laydown sale, we feel guilty for it being too easy. This hard-head way of thinking won't serve you well in the long run.

Ever see a sales guy who looks worn the fuck out? You know, the guy who's 40 years old, overweight, losing his hair and stressed out to the max? They go around talking about how stressful and hard sales is. It doesn't have to be that way. These are the guys who bring the stress on themselves by trying to sell people who aren't their ideal client.

Not everyone is a qualified prospect.

Let's talk about old-school sales for a minute. I'm talking cold calling and door knocking. When we are smilin' and dialin', we say things like "One out of every 100 people I talk to will buy from me." You do realize that means you wasted 99% of your time talking to 99 people who had no interest in what you sell, right? Imagine if you only had to talk to that one person instead of the other 99 people. How much less stressful would your work day be?

Rejection is tough. I don't care how strong you are, how big your ego is, or how good you are at sales; rejection is taxing. When the prospect talks crazy to you, slams the door shut in your face, or hangs up on you, it takes a toll mentally. I've learned to use my sales skills to avoid rejection at all costs. Not like a scared little bitch, but like a pro who only sells to those willing to be sold to. When a salesman makes this shift, it's a game-changer for them.

It's time you stop trying to sell everyone you run into. This old-school way of thinking is the reason salespeople look so stressed and use substances to escape the grueling reality of being a professional mind changer. What if instead of being a mind changer, you were a problem solver and you only sold to people whose problems you could solve? How much better would your time selling be? When you only sell to qualified prospects, your quality of life increases while your stress levels decrease.

Again, only sell to prospects who are qualified to buy your products.

When I ask Realtors who they sell to, they say, "Anyone who wants to buy, sell or lease real estate." As soon as they finish saying this, I reply with "I have a $25,000 trailer home in Oklahoma that I need you to sell." It's at this point they usually say, "I don't sell trailers," or something like that. Yet, they've just told me they would sell to "anyone." This is where they are messing up. Their marketing is that they will sell to anyone, but when "anyone" hits them up, they don't want the sale. Or worse yet, they take the trailer home listing and then complain they hate working the deal.

It's time you stop trying to sell to anyone. You need to be clear on exactly who it is you can help. You see, the mind gets what it focuses on. When you get 100% clear on who it is that's your perfect customer, you can position your marketing with offers that only speak to that person. At the same time, this should naturally repel those you do not wish to do business with.

Imagine if you went to work for eight hours a day and only spoke to qualified prospects. Sure, not all of them would buy from you, but you'd be way more fulfilled, have way less stress and get a sense of relief that you're not being hung up on or having doors slammed in your face.

I used to try and close anyone at any time, but I grew out of that phase.

These days, I don't like wasting my time or working with people who aren't a perfect fit for what I do. This cuts down on complaints as well as increases productivity on my end. I only focus on helping people who already earn six figures a year and have some sort of success track record. Back when I used to work with anyone, I got stressed from the people who just didn't get it. Instead of fighting the battle every day, I simply stopped trying to close people who weren't a fit.

In 2013, I started running ads on Facebook. My first ad was to loan officers. It said, "If you're not closing at least $2 million a month in mortgages, I can help you get there." This was a sales pitch that any LO would take. Problem is, if you're not closing $2 million a month already, you probably don't have any money. Selling to broke people is the hardest way to make sales ever. Don't do it!

After a month of dealing with broke person after broke person, I switched my offer up. I changed it to "If you're closing a minimum of $2 million a month and you want to get to $5 million, I'm your guy." This slowed my lead flow WAY DOWN. I went from 30 leads a day to 5 leads a day. But out of those 5 leads, 3 or 4 would buy my shit. When I got 30 leads, only 1-2 had the cash to buy from me. This not only saved me time, but it aligned me with folks who could benefit the most from what I sold. See the difference? I got to work less (5 leads vs. 30), and I made more money. All because I quit trying to sell to unqualified prospects.

Here's what you need to do. You need to take time today and create your perfect prospect. Who is it that you can help the most, with the least amount of effort? Who is it that you know you can do business with and enjoy it? Who do you want to work with?

Take the time today to make a decision.

Even if you sell insurance, you might say things like "Everyone needs insurance. Therefore, everyone is my prospect." While everyone does need insurance, do you want to sell to the guy who has bad credit, two DWIs and is three months behind on his current insurance policy? No. Of course, you don't. No matter what it is you sell, you need to get clear on who it is you want to sell to. This changes the game and it will change your life. I promise.

Chapter 38:

5 Sales Positions That Won't Exist in the Next 10 Years

I already know this is going to be controversial AF. I'm prepared for any backlash. I'm also ready to say "I told you so" when I'm right. You can choose to ignore my words and get mad at me, or maybe, just maybe I'm onto something, and you should seriously consider a backup plan.

It's no secret the world doesn't think favorably about salespeople. Every damn movie about us portrays us as whoremongers who rip people off and blow all our cash. While that's the case for some of us, it's not the case for all of us. But the news never does a feature on how well a salesman closed a deal.

The news only features salespeople stealing, ripping people off and other fuckery.

Some of the most notorious sales positions are being phased out right now. I'm not saying it's right. I'm not jockeying for it either. I'm just pointing out the obvious facts and direction we are headed in for the near future. All I'm doing here is indicating trends that are looming and that are not going away. But the sales jobs behind them are.

1. Car Sales:

The general public does not think favorably about car salespeople. If you asked 10 people on the street what the shadiest sales industry is, nine would say car sales. The remaining one would say, "stockbroker." Pretty much all of us have been got by a car salesman. I used to sell cars; in all my years in sales, no one ever talked down to me like the people who bought cars from me. The public is not a big fan of car folks.

With companies like Carvana in existence, more and more manufacturers will turn to that model and eventually bypass the existing dealer model altogether. Look at Tesla. They sell direct from the OEM, and their sales staff will soon be non-existent, too. Right now, Tesla salesmen take clients on test drives. Now that Tesla's self-driving, that aspect won't even be needed anymore. Also, I believe in the future we won't own cars. We will simply hail self-driving cars from Uber to pick us up. We will be able to convert our garages into livable space.

2. Mortgage Sales:

This is my favorite group of salespeople on this list. I worked in mortgages from 2003 to 2010. I made a ton of money. I loved every bit of it. It's a fulfilling job. This is why it's hard for a lot of LOs to admit their time is coming to an end. I don't blame them; I didn't want to let go of my awesome job either. That doesn't change the obvious, though.

With new technology like Rocket Mortgage on the rise, the LO job will be gone in seven years tops. You have 3-5 good years left to take as much money as possible from the bank. They will be cutting you off as a LO soon. Let's be real; they have already cut the commission 3-4 times now. Bankers are greedy. The banks don't want to pay the LOs hundreds of thousands of dollars in commissions each year if they don't have to. This combination of big banker greed and technology equals a coming doomsday for LOs.

3. Insurance Sales:

To be honest, I'm not sure how insurance salespeople are still around. I get that the older agents have a book of business they manage, but new agents earn much less and really don't do much. My agent, God bless him, spends more time telling me to go online and fill stuff out than he does helping me. He keeps outsourcing his job to technology, not realizing it will soon replace him.

Insurance companies are among the richest companies in the world. They have the money and technology to pad their bottom line without paying commissions. We see this with Esurance and similar companies. Matter of fact, all insurance commercials point you to a website and not to a human to do business with them. This should be sending the signals that the salesman is no longer needed in the equation.

4. Phone/Cable Sales:

If you sell B2B or B2C hardwired phone systems, your time is coming to an end. With technologies like Google Voice and the rise of smartphones, the old-school phones will go away. According to Ray Kurzweil, we will be wearing all the communication devices we need soon. I seriously doubt we will be walking around carrying a big-ass business phone.

A lot of businesses these days rely on their network of smartphones instead of some overpriced, complicated phone system. It's so much easier to just use the phone you have on you constantly. Every time I go into a business, the only person I see using an old-school phone is the secretary at the front desk. Everyone else stares at their smartphones. Plus, people are talking less and less. Email and text are the preferred communication method these days.

5. Recruiting:

Third-party recruiters will soon go the way of the dinosaurs. Companies will use in-house technology and employees to recruit talent. The best recruiters I know work for the company they recruit for. They are not third-party recruiters. You can easily see the number one complaint on LinkedIn is recruiters. Recruiters annoy the shit out of people. Third-party recruiters are not seen as a necessity by high-level producers.

We live in a time where if you want a job somewhere, all you have to do is get online, apply and sell your way into the job. A recruiter and their network are no longer the only way to go. With companies like Glassdoor and Monster, you can go direct to the source without having to align with a third-party recruiter. This job is phasing out quicker than any of the above-listed jobs, too.

I'm not here to give you doom and gloom. I'm just a person who watches the trends, technology and the market all day, every day. This is what I do. The people I'm aligned with at *Forbes*, *Entrepreneur* and *Huffington Post* are saying the same thing.

I'm not just coming out of left field here with doomsday news. I'm simply reaffirming what smart people have been saying for years.

Here's my advice. Take it for what it is. If I were in any of these five industries, I'd either get out, or I'd work my ass off for the next five years and get all I can get. I'd wake up every day and act like if I didn't close sales I'd lose my job. I'd save all my money, and I'd start plotting my next move. All I'm doing here is looking out for you.

In the event I'm wrong (I'm not), you'll still have a great 5-year run. There's nothing wrong with that, is there?

Don't forget, you can always look for side income.

For instance, find ways to make more money in our BFA Entourage program: BreakFreeAcademy.com/Entourage.

About the Author

A BAMF, unafraid to take action, Ryan Stewman, aka the "Hardcore Closer," is a bestselling author, podcaster and blogger. Best known for consulting with Alpha personality types on rapidly growing their sales via the use of powerful advertising and marketing, Ryan is a salesman turned CEO. He has not had a salaried job his entire life. He's mastered the art of super effective communication and has closed more transactions than he has time to count. With his no-BS approach to strategizing and scaling businesses, Ryan has helped high-net-worth performers adjust their business plans resulting in windfall profits.

After gaining prolific social media experience, Ryan decided to teach people from all sales fields and industries how to sell online. In the first year, Break Free Academy (BFA) closed over $150K in gross sales; the second year BFA hit over $300K; in 2016, BFA generated over $2M and in 2017, BFA grossed $4M+.

His notoriety and savage sales acumen have put him on the pages of the largest media publications on the planet. He contributes to and has been featured in *Forbes, Entrepreneur, Addicted2Success, The Good Men Project, The Lighter Side of Real Estate* and the *Huffington Post* in addition to other top-tier sites.

He states the key to his success is doing the work.

HardcoreCloser.com is an online learning resource for salespeople, selling e-learning products in the advertising, marketing funnel sales and social media arenas and offers personal coaching and live events.

Break Free Academy is Hardcore Closer's flagship program and provides every tool needed to market businesses online and crush the competition.

Ryan was born and raised in Texas. He's a doting husband and proud father to three sons. He and his family live in Dallas.

Subscribe to his blog at www.HardcoreCloser.com